The American Father

The American Father

A New Approach to Understanding Himself, His Woman, His Child

William Reynolds

PADDINGTON PRESS LTD

NEW YORK & LONDON

Library of Congress Cataloging in Publication Data
Reynolds, William, 1928–
  The American Father – Himself, His Woman,
His Child.

  Bibliography: p.
  1. Fathers – United States.   2. Husband and
wife – United States.   3. Father and child.
4. Men – Psychology.   I. Title.
HQ756.R48   301.42'7   78–8951
ISBN 0 448 22917X

Filmset in England by Servis Filmsetting Ltd, Manchester
Printed and bound in the United States
Designed by Sandra Shafee

IN THE UNITED STATES
PADDINGTON PRESS
Distributed by
GROSSET & DUNLAP

IN THE UNITED KINGDOM
PADDINGTON PRESS

IN CANADA
Distributed by
RANDOM HOUSE OF CANADA LTD.

IN SOUTHERN AFRICA
Distributed by
ERNEST STANTON (PUBLISHERS) (PTY) LTD

IN AUSTRALIA AND NEW ZEALAND
Distributed by
A.H. & A.W. REED

Contents

For my parents,
for my children
and for Professor Kenneth W. Spence

Acknowledgments

I would like to express my deepest gratitude to Russell Freedman, my writing teacher at the New School, for his help and encouragement, and to Emma Dally, my editor at Paddington Press, for her skillful yet gentle editing.

Special thanks go to my wife, Leah, for her indispensable aid in clarifying concepts, and editing and typing the manuscript, and to those many people, fathers, mothers and children, who taught me so much while working with them.

New York, 1978

Preface

Being a father in America's consumer-minded society is not a glamorous image, nor, for that matter, does it bring forth even a sparkle in a world which seems to value visibility above all else. Indeed, there has been considerable concern lately that the role of father is sinking slowly away under the onslaught of complex changes in modern life. That concern is only further evidence that the premises upon which parenting today is based are not oriented to the male.

The man called Father in this book is a composite personality drawn from many men with widely differing backgrounds and personal styles. What all of these men hold in common is their maleness and their continuing, uniquely male motive to maintain their hold on the women they need.

While Father's personal style generally belongs to the white middle class, the male motivation reflected does not. Thus Father can be any of a number of different types: the corporation executive staring out the window on the 6.29 to Westport, or the local school janitor washing up to return home; the jovial, wise-cracking fellow on the first tee Saturday morning, or the pre-occupied, slightly drunk guy tarrying in the local bar long after dinnertime at home has come and gone; the harried-looking divorced father driving through the rain on a Sunday morning, already half an hour late to pick up his kids for the day, or the articulate young professional asking so many questions at meet-the-teacher night. Father could be any of these men, and more; his ethnic and racial identification only influences the ways he expresses his needs but not the needs themselves.

Whether his wife works or not influences his strategies and, of course, the circumstances of his life, but not his most fundamental motivation. We are reminded at every turn these days of the vast changes taking place around us, and of the many implications these changes have for men. It is the theme of this book that these changes are more apparent than real and that while the words describing the life goals of men may change, their needs and the basic pattern of their lives remain the same.

Fathering, in fact, is a secondary interest to Father who is primarily occupied with the torments and rewards of being Mother's lover first and foremost. His children are seldom the center of his life and a good many of his dealings with them are influenced more by his feelings at the moment about Mother than anything in particular the children may be doing.

The opening chapters of the book examine Father as he is: a male, and Mother's lover. His male needs are not quite the same as Mother's despite the current fervor for homogenizing the sexes in motivation as well as in goals and skills. His relationship with his own mother insures the difference. Differences in motivation often make his behavior obscure and maddening to Mother who feels she needs her energy for more productive pursuits than just attending to his whims. That Father often persists in aggravating Mother in a thousand different ways often earns him the diagnosis of "immature" by today's healthy-living experts as well as by Mother herself.

The middle chapters survey the lovers' life together. Even in their early times together, when they argue about trust and communication, sex and each other's family, "getting it together" turns out to be difficult on any consistent basis, and they both find themselves irritable and out of sorts far more than they ever dreamed. When the first child arrives, stresses are placed on their relationship which are difficult to cope with with any degree of harmony and prove too great for many. Their marriage disintegrates for reasons both sides are at a loss to adequately explain, and divorces are sometimes completed without either one really knowing what happened. The survivors march ahead to further children, further problems with each other sometimes, further marriages and a fair amount of competitiveness about other family members.

Father does have some very basic feelings and attitudes about two areas of his life, in addition to Mother – his work and his child. Father's degree of involvement with his work generally turns out to be very strong, at least when he's there. Often at home, however, Father is prone to reporting only the stress and fatigue and none of the joys. Mother, just now making big inroads into career life, is not sure she's too thrilled to hear about the bleakness and strain of work. She might also resent such whining if her only prospects are to stay at home and look after the children. As for the children, Father has some strong feelings for them too except that in practice he has a difficult job untangling them from his current mood about Mother, and when their marriage goes through the inevitable hard times and other loves appear on the scene, they go about adultery in such different ways, pursuing such different goals. Late divorce comes to quite a few, but even then the results are often bitter and inconclusive about who loved whom more, or enough, or not at all.

The concluding chapters of the book review the assumptions of America's current philosophy about parenting which emphasizes activism and visibility in the child's life. That these standards of what comprises a "good" parent, consciously or otherwise, overtly make Father look bad would merely be unfortunate until it is considered that these same standards define what good mental health is all about these days. Because his basic male motivation and experiences often make him awkward and uncomfortable in the winner's circle of today's parenting sweepstakes, Father finds that family living has, in some respects at least, pushed him into hard and guilty times. If Father is determined not to play by the contemporary rules of exemplary parenting, then there are a few ideas for him to consider which may make fathering a bit easier and, God forbid, more fun.

1

After all, He is My Father

The American father is so often that man about whom his grown children say, "Well, I love him, of course. After all, he is my father. But I never really got to know him." He is that silent, apparently remote man who seems to participate so grudgingly and erratically in family life: the family mute who is typically characterized as moody, angry, "closed," or, at best, as merely reserved. And it gets worse. He is often seen as having no positive feelings at all, or, if they are present, as being unable to express them, poor fellow, because as a boy he was taught that it is unmasculine to show one's softer feelings. Mental-health professionals and feminists in particular seem fascinated with this glib but naive proposition.

Whether Father is recalled as a stern and humorless man or as one on the easy-going and gregarious side, there is always a hint of inaccessibility about him and an interest in family proceedings that is a sometimes thing. The means by which Father creates that aura of inaccessibility vary, but the usual ones are television watching, sleeping, newspaper reading or simply by not being there at all. Father is also regarded as a rather solitary creature, with none of the close and enduring friendships which so typify his wife, and his frequent silences at home make him particularly perplexing and unnerving. Touchingly, so many growing children believe it is only *their* father who is like that, only *their* father who must be exposed to public view with apprehension and uncertainty, whose moods create instant tension in the home like a ticking bomb.

The children do not regard Mother and Father as lovers and accordingly see them as individuals, or parents, with little in the way of any real flavor to their relationship. This is especially true of Father, who seldom reveals himself to the children or sheds any light on his most absorbing concern – Mother and his place in her life. Most certainly the children, whether five years old or fifty, never come close to making any connection between Father's behavior and Mother's. But then, unfortunately, Mother frequently misses the connection herself.

Father, however, sees it all quite differently, to say the least. He sees himself as an intense and loving man, even passionate and romantic, waging a constant inner struggle against his fears of insignificance to Mother and the world at large. Father is perplexed by envy as he compares his own amorphous role with the generally satisfying one that motherhood has created for his wife. Father is frustrated and isolated by the constant urging these days to express his "real" feelings, ones in fact which he seldom has, like loneliness and depression, while there is no place for him to express the kinds of feelings he has in abundance: angry, competitive, violent and sexually eccentric. Nobody, but nobody, wants to hear that stuff.

The common image of Father as an ineffective, unfeeling, inarticulate boor seems to enjoy great popularity in the current society where interpersonal relations are conducted entirely by ear. The mental health folks and every genus of growth guru urge Father to improve his ability to "communicate": try to banish those demons of restrictive childhood training and let your real feelings come out. There doesn't seem to be the slightest doubt in their minds that those feelings are in there, so the key to better living lies in expanding the frequency and range of the spoken word. Life is a vocabulary test.

And in this era of divorce and general marital malfunction, when things go wrong between Mother and Father the disaster is, sure enough, ascribed to a "failure of communication," rather than to the simpler but less exotic notion that some people have trouble paying attention to what is right before their eyes and that others in their anger are prone to doing the damnedest things. Perfecting the absurd, relationship specialists testify with assurance that the communication problems are brought about by vast changes in personal development and role definition.

Communication between Father and Mother can in fact be letter perfect, except that it is generally executed in different styles and directed at drastically different goals. Father's style with Mother is commonly non-verbal, emphasizing action and aimed at keeping Mother's head turned his way; Mother's style is verbal, puts little stress on action and is designed to keep Father functioning happily in a particular role. Father is not one for talking, while Mother is not one for seeing; the blind and the mute play to a tie, where both sides lose.

The quality commonly attributed to energetic verbal communication in marriage is that it makes life and the relationship more meaningful and complete. While that may be esthetically true, from Father's practical and purely male point of view the result of verbalization appears to be that it makes life easier for everybody. As it turns out, making life easier for Mother is often the very last thing on Father's mind. When life gets easier for Mother, Father gets nervous. He becomes uneasy and apprehensive, and finally the fear that he is losing something of the most urgent importance to him makes him angry. Just why this should be the case stems from a basic behavioral fact.

The single most powerful force in determining how Father relates to his child is Father's need for the mother of that child. The opposite of this, however, is not true: Mother's need for Father is seldom the major factor in shaping her relationship with her child. An appreciation of this fundamental sexual discrepancy is essential to any understanding of Father's role as it has been, as it is, or as it might be in the future. Fathering is not a process which can make much sense simply as a relationship between an adult male and a child, and nothing more. Father is a man and lover first, and a father second, with his goals and rewards therefore tipped in certain directions. For Mother, her various roles as wife, mother, daughter and friend are not only more equal in strength, but are far better integrated into her life.

This key sexual difference is what accounts for the common observation that following separation or divorce, Father's relationship with the kids tends to drift somewhere between placid indifference and outright abandonment, while Mother's remains as intense and involved as during the marriage. Father often blames the development of this distance on the usual custody arrangement which places the children with Mother, but this is only a convenient, apparently plausible explanation for an otherwise inexplicable disengagement. The kids often fear that they will lose Father following a break-up of the family, and they are usually right, despite attempts to reassure them. Divorced Father is seldom a major active factor in his child's life, and the reason lies not in custody or visitation arrangements, but at a far more basic emotional level: his primary ties to the child have been severed.

When Mother, therefore, drifts too far from being Father's lover, that's when Father loses his temper and dummies up, among other things. Father usually knows from boyhood that silence enrages those who take it as a personal affront, causing them to rush at the silent one, expending great amounts of energy and time to gouge out the reason for the silence. Silence, as we shall see, is usually Father's last defense against total obliteration by Mother, the kids and the world.

Father is doubted these days within a society whose values of "good" parenting are premised on a model of frenzy and activism which insures that Father will finish last and that Mother can readily see herself and the kids as the chronic victims of his sloth and indifference. The ever-present experts seem satisfied with their peculiar belief that Father as a man is simply an inarticulate version of Mother. The flaming vanguard of the women's movement is optimistically investigating the idea that, with a few critical advances in biochemistry, Father and his accursed organ might be dispensed with altogether. In short, America is not exactly enthusiastic about Father and rarely attempts a realistic look at him; the emphasis is always on Father as he *ought* to be rather than on as he is.

But Father is very much a flesh-and-blood creature with needs and motives of his own. His behavior is very consistent with those needs, although it often appears inconsistent and incomprehensible to others. His children's vision of him, for example, is descriptively accurate, but their view is forever flawed when they try to give meaning to his behavior. The meaning of Father's behavior is hard to grasp not only for his children, but in the community of experts as well, where there exists a strong reliance on the spoken word and the demand that everyone explain himself.

Let's visit with some of Father's grown-up children as they recall that man they once called Daddy, although that was not his real name.

Grown Children Remember Their Fathers

There are relatively few adults around who do not have a more vivid and detailed recollection of Mother as an individual than of Father. Regardless of what Mother's specific temperament might have been, she was usually the more visible of the two and regarded as easier to know. The children invariably believe that because they spent so much more time with Mother, it is only natural for them to know her better. In addition, Mother seems to have a more spirited need to talk about herself and her feelings to the kids, but her reasons, to be explained later, are far more complicated than they appear, certainly to the children.

Recalling Mother and Father as a couple is more difficult, even for astute children. Their recollections have the sound of unreality about them, even when the main characters are singular and easily describable as individuals. Some of the trouble is plainly produced by the child's inability to experience Mother

and Father as lovers. It seems beyond the human reach to acknowledge that Mom and Dad ever had nights of intensity and
urgency, sweating and moaning, as heaven came briefly within
reach of their bed. Despite the alleged liberation of recent times,
college-age children of the lovers remain insufferably priggish in
their dismissal of any such possibility. Even for those who recall
from childhood the sounds of creaking beds and the indistinct
murmurs in the night wafting through the walls, the sounds tend
to be dissociated from the people, and perhaps, after all, it's best
to forget them.

Another part of the difficulty in recalling Mother and Father
as a couple, however, stems from a certain elusiveness in Father.
To many children it is clear that Father didn't take much time or
trouble to make himself known to them. The major factor
influencing the perception of Father is whether or not the child
had any experience with him away from home and Mother. If
so, the man who appeared abroad was often dramatically
different, and both Fathers, at home and outside, were far from
the common television staple of Father as a benign jerk who
suffers criticism with a resigned tolerance and is always eventually
willing to learn from Mother and the kids.

For those grown children who saw Father only at home with
Mother, their view of him is startlingly similar to Mother's and
to the vision of him they held as growing children. That impression continues into adulthood, and the emphasis is on Father as
an apparent personality type. Their favorite word to describe
Father is "moody," followed by "quiet." His moods, which
created a degree of uncertainty, were never connected to anything in particular. He was just plain moody. A grown daughter
in her thirties puts it succinctly:

> We never knew what to expect from my Dad. Usually he was pretty
> quiet and didn't say all that much to us. I remember sometimes he
> was fun and played with us. Other times he'd be in a real bad mood,
> and my sisters and I just steered clear of him. We just never knew.

The children learned to read Father's famous moods as a matter of self-interest, namely, their safety. Accordingly, their approaches to him and overall behavior around him were largely regulated, consciously or not, by Father's mood barometer.

Another daughter recalls something else strange about Father:

> My father never seemed to have an opinion of his own, one way or another, about us. He'd just say, "Do what your mother tells you," and then he'd go back to his paper, and that would be that. If we argued that Mom wasn't being fair, he'd just get irritated and say, "That's between you and your mother." But late at night sometimes I'd hear them fighting about us, and I swear I could never understand that.

Did this mean that Father simply had no active interest in the kids? Did it mean that Father had such sublime faith in Mother's judgment that for him to express his opinion to the kids would be redundant and silly? Then why the fights later? Or did it mean that such episodes were pieces of a strange choreography between Mom and Dad, with the kids merely the chorus striving to understand the intrinsically obscure?

While Father seldom seemed to make any deliberate effort to reveal his inner life to the kids, Mother often did it for him. Sometimes the motive was revenge, as in the following situation involving a divorce recalled by a systems analyst in his thirties:

> My parents were divorced when I was about seven. My mother was always telling me what a selfish and dishonest man my father was and that went on for years. Whenever I was with my father, I would sometimes be looking for dishonest things he might do, almost like I was trying to catch him at something bad.

This story of divorce is rather typical. Children of divorce suffer not so much from the divorce itself, but from their inability to get either parent or both ever to shut up about it.

Even when the Mother-Father connection seemed to the children to be more solid and stable, Mother was still the in-house interpreter of Father's feelings, especially about the children. A forty-ish professional man recalls his father from this perspective:

My father hardly ever spoke directly to any of us. He was pretty quiet. When I was in college, I asked my mother how my father felt about us. I guess I was really asking how he felt about me. Mom told me how proud he was of us and that he loved us so much. I asked her why he never said it to us, and she said that was just his way.

This is a common theme when Father is recalled: Father tells Mother, and Mother tells the kids. Even when Father was critical of the children, it was often Mother who delivered the bad news to the troops. The child's view, even at age forty, is that Father was simply that way, just as Mother was the way she was. There is seldom the slightest suspicion that something more may have been involved in all of that circuitous communication. The children always believe that that was Mother's and Father's way of dealing with them, and nothing more. If Father was critical about the kids, then it must mean just that; surely it couldn't be that Dad was really attacking Mom where he felt she was vulnerable, and would have looked for something to criticize, even had the kids been perfect angels.

Another scenario of a similar type would have Mother regularly unburdening herself, especially to a particular child, usually the eldest, with the major theme being her trouble with Father. Another grown daughter, nearing forty, recalled it this way:

My mother used to confide in me all the time about her problems with my father. I can remember it even when I was very little, like eight or nine. She'd always tell me when there was some new thing, but usually it was pretty much the same things. She would cry a lot, and I remember when I was in high school, I told her she should leave him several times. But she said she just couldn't do that to us.

Is this merely a sensitive and compassionate child reacting to the heartbreak of a tormented Mother, or was Mother a bit more profit-oriented than that? This woman's brother characterized the same Mother as a "martyr," apparently satisfied that this diagnosis puts it all to rest, but maybe missing the real nature of some of Mother's most competitive strivings.

Sometimes both Father and Mother would get into martyred competition and Father would tell his own story to the kids so as not to be outdone by Mother. A talented social worker in her thirties remembers having not only Father translated for her but the entire marriage by both parties:

> I felt sorry for both my parents although they made a pretty good marriage after all. My father told me his real love was the sea but he couldn't continue at it after he married my mother and had a child. My mother said she was really in love with another man but he was killed in the war, and she just happened to meet my father at around that time and knew he was a pretty good guy.

Many grown children remember Father fighting a lot with Mother. What they fought about was sometimes familiar, like the kids themselves, but at other times was obscure and puzzling, though just as unpleasant. "You name it, and they'd fight about it," was the comment of one young man recalling his parents in a mid-western suburb. Often the lovers fought about little things, seemingly odd things to generate so much heat, and the kids became convinced that Mom and Dad were just poorly matched.

Almost all grown children have some interesting memories of Father on the subject of visitors. When Sonny or Sis were having friends in, they could usually count on Mother being pretty civil and often downright charming, at least if the visitors were the right kind of friends. Father, on the other hand, was a different matter, depending on those moods again. The key question before many junior social events was, "Is Father going to be home?" When guests were visiting Mom and Dad, the same uncertain theme might well be repeated. Mother was noted as quite nice at such times, often plainly exuberant in her hostess role. Even Father sometimes became sociable and less fearsome and, with the proper amount of alcohol he could become exceptionally friendly, even funny or clever. The kids always knew that these were excellent opportunities to ask for money or permission for dubious ventures. But at other times. . . . Well, let's hear about those from a graduate student in his twenties:

Sometimes they would have people over for dinner, and my father would get up and go inside to turn on the TV. My mother would be running in every five minutes to get him, and you could see on her face how mad she was. No kidding, he would just get right up and leave everybody sitting there.

After his social appearances, even the better ones, Father would be moodier than ever when the guests departed. Often he would raise a hell of a fuss with Mother on the very next day. The kids figured he was just tired from the party or had a hangover.

In most recollections of Father at home, he is commonly remembered as moody and quiet, with his intermittent surliness or participation difficult to connect to any specific events or circumstances. In most cases, the kids' appraisal of Father tends to approximate Mother's, and later in life the children are often found still commiserating with Mother for her courage and patience in hanging in there doggedly in the face of uncertain rewards. The children see little sense in Father's behavior and often conclude that Dad really missed out on a lot in life; and they do not doubt that Mother's life is as unrewarding as it seems to be out front.

Some of Father's children, however, do get a look at him in circumstances away from home and Mother, and the experience is often confusing and unsettling. These novel glimpses generally occur around Father's place of employment or in some dealings with his cronies. A son of thirty-two reported the following version of such an incident which is typical of such encounters:

I must have been seventeen the first time I saw my father away from our family. On this particular day I had to wait for him outside of where he worked to drive home with him. He came out with some other men, and they were laughing. They stood around for a few minutes, and my father was very funny – he was making them laugh. The other men seemed to really like him. I could hardly believe the whole thing – he was so different than I had ever seen him. I couldn't say a word to him. I thought I'd ask my mother about it later, but then I changed my mind.

The sudden mellowing that Father's temperament seems to undergo away from Mother is naturally ascribed by the child to another mysterious "mood." Mother makes that interpretation herself, as in this brief encounter reported by another of Father's grown daughters:

> Once in the summer while I was in high school, my father went to work without his briefcase. My mother asked me to take it to him at his office. It was the first time I'd ever been there. We went out for a sandwich and had the best time. He still didn't say all that much to me, but he was so nice and seemed really interested in what I was talking about. He said we'll have to do this again, but we never did. I told Mom about how friendly Dad had been, and she said he must be in a good mood.

Do these retrospective vignettes suggest that Father reserves his most noxious antics especially for Mother, and incidentally for the kids, at home? They certainly do, and the meaning of these encounters goes quite beyond the fact that Father is often less than candid about how much he suffers at work. The child is seeing a "different" man when he is outside, almost a stranger, and the discrepancy between this image and the one at home often provokes some disturbing thoughts. Years later the grown child may reflect wistfully on how nice it might have been to live with that stranger.

Mother herself often gets a look at the same stranger through a different medium: the telephone. Mother reports that Father frequently calls her from work during the day. Once he determines what her exact movements have been, an apparently idle exercise which, in fact, has the utmost significance to him, he sounds soft and pleasant, even romantic on occasion. Father truly misses Mother during the day, and Mother's morale leaps up several notches. But later, on the way home, some mysterious things begin to happen as he gets closer and closer to her, and he arrives home with his surliness at full sail. Mother is confused, and she wonders what has happened in the meantime to bring this on again. Nothing has happened. Father has simply been being a male again, and he's found, as he always can, some tiny item or other which has stoked the fires of his anger. Mother and Father sometimes live for months with their only soft and affectionate exchanges occurring on the telephone.

The upshot of it all is that Father is often seen as simply perverse by the people closest to him at home. This may be descriptively accurate, but the dynamics of the moodiness and perversity remain far from common understanding. Today's scholars are in no great hurry to examine the real needs, motives or rewards of men because one ends up facing stuff that is not very popular these days. Father's true needs are immediately indictable by the mental-health establishment as needs we should all want to see go away. All current views of Father, in fact, are greatly influenced by the healthy-living folks who insist on portraying Father as a misfit person, rather than as a male.

Experts in Living Look at Men

The marketing of mental health has become a major industry in America, and there is scarcely a citizen anywhere who hasn't been psychologized to some degree. Every avenue of the media has at least one of its own resident experts regularly pumping out wisdom and advice to the millions. What has emerged from this torrent of words are the collective standards of healthy living applied to every variety of creature. The theme of mentally-healthy living has suffused the popular consciousness at every level, and hardly any discussion of life can be held without implicitly referring to the current opinions of the experts. The healthy-living industry is divided into four basic areas: children, parenting, relationships and self-help.

The child business has had heavy play for some time now, made popular by the rise of public education as an art form, divorce as the modern curse of childhood, and the use of drugs which, according to some, will bring down the entire civilization. The marketing by experts and hucksters alike is done on a threat-and-crisis basis as each new half-decade uncovers fresh demons to strike down the fragile little ones: teenage gangs, the working mother, divorce, bottle feeding, drugs, alcohol, sexual ignorance, permissive schools, decline in religious attendance, and the absent father, to name but a few. It seems miraculous that there is a child left standing and still functioning; surely it is only a matter of time before a new book shows that not doing one's homework in the fifth grade causes cancer.

Closely allied is the parenting enterprise which dresses up good and evil parenting in spanking new costumes for daily examination. The parenting business reviews all the pitfalls of childhood, with heavy emphasis on the current ones, and its basic thrust is to set forth the millions of things a good parent can do to save Sonny and Sis from various devils, including themselves. For people with plenty of anxious energy, the complex route along which to steer the child is plotted, complete with the precise language with which to address him, and the ultimate rewards are projected with certainty. Of course, some space is always reserved for a sad, head-wagging look at those slackers who simply don't care enough about their children even to try good parenting.

The relationship industry has also received a great deal of coverage in recent years and features some of the same energetic activism found in the "How-to" country of parenthood. The difference lies in the beneficiary of this energy-expenditure and enthusiastic tinkering. When it is one's soul-mate who needs shaping-up, the stated objective is no longer mental health as it is with children, but better and happier living for all. It's hard to argue with those goals, and the relationship experts provide abundant clues to distinguish the good guys from the bad guys without fear of error.

The self-help business is at least as busy and profitable as the others, probably more so. In years gone by, Dale Carnegie types tackled this area and called it how to present oneself with confidence to other people. In those days Father himself was the top consumer of confidence transfusions. Since then, however, the theme has become less aggressive, more personal, and more concentrated on what to do about being alone and on the sickening implications of solitude. Never mind what anybody says, love yourself and be a beautiful person; this is the essential sermon of the self-help industry. Because they have developed the "cures" so thoroughly, the self-help crowd has necessarily defined what the adult diseases are so as to fit the treatments snugly.

Regardless of which area of the healthy-living business is involved, men generally, and Father most specifically, come off as the heavy. This systematic interpretation makes sense when one considers that Mother is the primary consumer for mental-hygiene marketing, and it would be poor judgment, to say the least, to offend one's best customer. Women consume advice and guidance products at the rate of about four-to-one compared with men. Father seldom pays attention to these things and has serious reservations about mental-health experts in the first place. Sometimes he is able to articulate his mistrust of Mother's reliance on the media scholars, but often he simply feels out of his element, without being able to identify why.

When the subject is children, for example, experts of every persuasion stress Sonny's and Sis's need for parental involvement in just about every facet of their existence. The children as depicted in the health books tend to be unisexual through adolescence and beyond, with boys and girls showing the same needs and coping with the same environments. The fact, however, that boys outnumber girls some four or five to one, in behavioral problems of every kind, including hyperactivity, learning disabilities, juvenile delinquency and acting out problems, remains ominously unexplained and usually unacknowledged. Perhaps this disturbing ratio will eventually produce a new, asymmetrical principle of mental health which may even indicate new shortcomings in Father previously unanalyzed.

When the context is "How-to-Parent," Father's stock drops even lower on the board. Busy, busy, busy, say the experts, that's what a good parent should be. The contemporary standards of healthy parenting, therefore, invariably demand a mildly hysterical level of energy which, for special occasions, can be kicked upward to absolute frenzy. Mother is the clear winner here, not only in the direct Virtue Points produced by "participating" in the child's life, but also by means of a substantial increase in the Victim Ratio, as she and the experts sadly agree that, yes, Father has indeed failed miserably here. The kids haven't had a "real" father, you know, and it's been only Mother's valiant, almost superhuman efforts in the breach which have saved the kids from complete annihilation of the human spirit.

Father does make a deliciously visible villain. In today's world, children in the home are regarded as creatures to be trained, developed, shaped and, if necessary, twisted into forms of life acceptable and even admirable to the outside world. The modern word for all of this heavy-handed training is "guidance," which connotes a touch of emotional sophistication blended with a healthy pinch of intellectual substance. The experts in How-to country have given the official carte blanche for every variety of tinkering, intervention and pressure on the child, inevitably calling it participation.

In his natural condition as a male, Father is not enthusiastic about all this guidance and participation, and has no gut grasp of the standards of judgment involved. Accordingly, Father has become the perfect bad guy for the How-to-Parent business, where the experts are always seeking new ways of helping Mother get Father "interested" in the children. To make this package sell, it is necessary, of course, to see the children as complete fools and potentially worse. The assumption that all of this interest and participation is the source of mental health remains blithely unquestioned.

In this alien context, the best diagnosis that Father can hope for concerning his lack of interest is that he is "immature." And what is mature? It means a condition of life which is apparently selfless, responsible to the point of morbidity, altruistic beyond any credible degree, and totally free of any nonsensical and absurd behavior; in short, utterly martyred. As we shall see, Father is often nonsensical and absurd and clearly over his head in the parenthood maturity league. "Boys will be boys" is interesting folk wisdom, but sooner or later he is expected to cast aside that random, reckless foolishness and take on the responsibilities of manhood with grim resolve. Father's general inability to make this transition at least on the sooner side becomes a continuing dilemma for him, and a considerable amount of his adult energy is spent desperately concealing the fact that he hasn't grown up and isn't sure he wants to.

It is in the promotion of the relationship business, however, that Father has taken his most telling lumps as a male. Mother is just as avid a consumer of relationship tracts and lectures as she is of child-and-parent wisdom, with pretty much the same results. Relationships mean feelings, and feelings, which obviously are meant to be expressed, are sold these days on a unisex basis. We are all just human beings, right? All of us have the same feelings and desires, right? So let's just be open and honest with each other about our feelings and get it together, right? But Father is a male, not just a person, and he does not have the same feelings, desires or objectives as Mother, nor is he likely to have them in this lifetime.

The result is that Father and Mother find their relationship rather stormy, with the blame normally landing on Father for being a closed person who simply refuses to own up to his feelings. The experts agree and blame society, thereby confirming Mother's conviction that Father has been warped by his childhood training in masculinity. Were it not for that harsh and repressive experience, Father would be ready and willing to show his real feelings, which would be pretty much like Mother's, including her capacity to cry, alone or with others. It all sounds so simple and plausible; it diagnoses Father and identifies all of the bad guys. Neat packaging.

The mental-health experts are as seriously devoted to the value of verbalization as Mother is, but for somewhat different reasons. We are mainly men who have been reasonably feminized by all those years in school; the basic business of university life is to place huge premiums on reading and talking, with very little emphasis on action. Also, our pursuit of psychotherapy has given us a regard for the spoken word previously found only in drama majors. Psychotherapy is a devilishly difficult trade if the client isn't much of a talker, and really poor verbalizers are labeled resistant or uncooperative, depending on the theory. When the cure fails entirely, the patient is blamed because he isn't motivated to help himself.

Our experience in the legitimate concerns of mental health tends to make us excessively clinical and, if given half a chance, many will diagnose any behavior at fifty paces. In recent times, to the profound embarrassment of the health professions, some of our most eminent experts have given evaluations by the carload of famous murderers, politicians and assorted blackguards, sight unseen. When dispensing advice to the millions, our language invariably ends up liberally laced with proscriptives like *should* and *ought*.

The experts are also taught to speak in jargon, and to jargonize comes to serve a special need: how else can one demonstrate the uniqueness of one's thoughts? Jargon creates impressions in others, and one impression is always that the subject under discussion is far more complex than it might appear, or, freely translated, I'm smarter than you are. After a few years of such training and experience, many experts in the social and behavioral sciences are entirely unable to express themselves without the jargon. Eventually this rarefied language infiltrates the applied areas like education, business and, of course, healthy living. The meaning of all such language on any level remains obscure, but it creates the illusion of authority and understanding so often mistaken for active intelligence.

For these reasons, the ability for verbal expression comes to be the highest civilized achievement for the experts and this happily coincides with Mother's belief that her propensity for talking is a profound natural asset. To talk is healthy, and to express one's real feelings verbally is the very apex of health. Indeed, now that we are becoming interested in death and dying, it can safely be predicted that there will soon be an officially healthy way to die, which naturally will have the patient offering his last emotional testament loud and clear, to the relief of the family and the pleasure of the staff. Those who enter that dark tunnel in silence will go mildly rebuked for not venting their real feelings, whatever they might be at that utterly isolated moment.

The combination of the verbal criterion of mental health, the unisex view of personal feelings and the conviction that Father has been ravaged by his childhood training in how to be a man unites to diagnose Father ipso facto as unhealthy, a kind of emotional, second-class citizen. The simple conclusion from this is that Father is forced to withhold the expression of his feelings, presumed to be identical to Mother's, which, if only released, would bring the two of them together in the final blessed relief of shared feelings and tearful union. The incentive, therefore, to liberate Father's feelings is irresistable. The marriage-counseling therapist purrs professionally, "Let's get our feelings out on the table; let's just let it all hang out." To the dismay and frustration of all, Father usually dodges and demurs.

Father is withholding his feelings all right, but for vastly different reasons than those so slickly noted, reasons actually far removed from that harrowing masculine training so dear to the hearts of the blame-placers. And the feelings he is withholding would, in truth, draw little if any admiration or relief from either Mother or the professionals, and for the very best of reasons: they aren't very much like Mother's after all. Unfortunately for many, Father is a male and is quite different from Mother in several vital emotional and motivational respects.

The fourth major area of modern wisdom, the self-help industry, demonstrates perfectly how poorly Father fits the mold for the currently fashionable diseases. Father is considered unhealthy by the experts because of his reluctance to communicate, but on the other hand, he is not suffering from the major interpersonal ills currently being attested to so vigorously. Strange business, this.

Dozens of self-improvement books appear each year with varying slants on what we as human beings *should* be, *might* be or *ought* to be: "potential," to the sophisticates. Each one has its own version of cute little word games to help us search out those pesky pockets of bad feeling and self-reproach. The message is always the same, however phrased, about getting it together, liking and loving yourself, and so on, and the message is this: you don't need other people to tell you that you are beautiful and whole; learn to do it yourself. Why, it can even be fun, by golly. What is the disease all this spiritual cheerleading is designed to cure?

Loneliness, of course. The book-jacket blurbs snarl out at us that loneliness is the scourge of modern living. Big cities, nuclear families, alienation and all that, you know. We are all twisted and bent from the cramps of human abandonment and disinterest. It is oppressive loneliness which drives women, even divorced or widowed Mother, into the sexual slaughter of the singles joint, looking for Mister Right, only to awaken later sexually used and emotionally ravished by insincere and shallow men, some of them, curse the bastards, even married. As close as the writings on loneliness come to self-parody, the phenomenon itself is very real. No self-improvement formula can reach this disease, because it is too true and too malignant for Band-aids. The stunning reality of the pain and the tears is not likely to be relieved by consolation prizes.

Many a father's daughter cries the nights away because she is alone and doesn't "have anybody." Even when she does, she sometimes still cries because it shouldn't be like it is – so terribly alone. The sobs can come anywhere without warning, shopping on a Saturday afternoon, watching children at play in a park, passing an elderly couple slowly promenading with clasped hands, anywhere. The loneliness determines every aspect of her weekly schedule, to prevent being left alone to think.

Father is seldom lonely. It isn't something he hides or suppresses; he simply doesn't suffer from it much. If he is one of the relative few who do, he attempts to remedy it the same way that Mother does, by rounding up some people to keep him company. Failing that, he will talk away on the telephone to whomever can be located, almost anybody will do. The cure for Mother's loneliness is the approval of another person who cares and by whose presence her basic worth in life is validated and confirmed. In self-help country that is not enough. One must not only accept oneself, but like oneself, even love oneself, for the final approval. What emotional chaos this must cause the literal-minded can only be imagined.

Mother's magazines routinely confirm the devastation of the loneliness disease and acknowledge her victimization by it in clever yet stereotyped ways. Once granted the legitimate horror of it, Mother is exhorted to find something good in the suffering, something that will improve her as a human being – a Great Books course perhaps, maybe some meditation exercises to get her into her real inner self, or, for the truly ambitious, a specific program to develop herself into a terrific person. Once the possible happy endings are covered, the blame must be placed where it belongs, on the insensitive, narrow, unfeeling men, present or absent, living or dead. Father's magazines, on the other hand, are taking up the advantages of the triple-option offense for the Dallas Cowboys or showing ever-more vivid photos of the naked female body, wherein nowadays the vagina is shot from so close that some momentary confusion with open-heart surgery is inadvertently created.

In recent times, a spate of books has appeared identifying an even more vicious human misfortune: "depression," son, or daughter, of loneliness. The expert authors argue that frighteningly large numbers of us are prone to sinking into a morass of gloom and sadness at an early age. The cause? Well, it's a kind of anger turned inward as self-rejection because of lack of approval or feelings of some sort of failure in life, producing reactions of worthlessness and hopelessness. What's the cure? Some intimate personal contact with others helps, and talking about it, of course, to an accepting and sympathetic listener will make one feel a good deal better. In other words, both depression and loneliness are states whose core condition is the absence of an approving other person.

Who are the victims? In fact, Mother is again the major casualty by far; Father, as a male, is seldom depressed. Like all major emotional ills, depression is a rare phenomenon, and truly depressed people have little desire to eat or even to go to the bathroom, much less talk about it to anybody. They really don't give a damn about anything, and they certainly are not out buying magazines off the newsstands. Father has his moments of depression, just as he has his moments of loneliness, but neither lasts very long or influences his behavior with any consistency. Father's male motivation doesn't fit comfortably into the passive posture required for both loneliness and depression.

If Father as a man is not lonely and not depressed, then what the devil is he? Usually he's angry to some degree, sometimes mildly, sometimes in a flat-out rage. Occasionally he's not mad at all. But he sometimes says he's lonely or depressed, doesn't he? True, but what Father says he does or doesn't feel and the actual state of his emotions are often two different things entirely. In his personal testimony Father turns out to be a poor witness.

Why Father's natural and most common negative state of life is anger rather than the loss-of-approval conditions like loneliness and depression makes for an absorbing and complex story of male motivation and striving. Father is not merely an inarticulate version of Mother after all; he is really quite different in a few ways that would just about guarantee some difficulty in communication and living, even if he and Mother were all-out honest in every respect. Honesty by itself is not the key to understanding the Father-Mother connection, despite all the current advice to the contrary. It is the acceptance of the differences between them as men and women which unlocks the tangle in their union, even if that union falls inevitably short of the promised land of Super-oneness painted with such flourishes by today's Love Doctors.

2

Father and Mother: the Tragicomic Lovers

Once a child or two is on the premises and the gains have been counted, Father reports a gathering sense of loss. It's a very personal thing, this feeling of loss, and it isn't entirely attributable to the more obvious factors one might blame, such as aging, or loss of sex appeal.

It's not really the kids either – or at least not directly. Even if he convinces himself that he's completely selfless when it comes to the kids, as is fashionable these days, the nagging sense of loss will persist. Nor is it any straightforward envy of the children with Father wishing he were they; he has plenty of jealousy, as we'll see, but it's not from him begrudging their youth or the lives they have created. There are always interpretations of Father being jealous of a son or even a daughter but those accounts are usually written by somebody's grown child still angrily flattering themselves about the extent of their narcissistic powers.

Father's sense of loss is also not explicable by the dramatic decline of esteem that the "father image" has allegedly suffered in recent times. Yes, to be a father these days is to be seen as rather a feckless turkey who either spends too much time at work, thereby making the family suffer, or who doesn't spend that much time at work but still adamantly refuses to become involved with the local School Committee for In-Toilet Surveillance by Closed-Circuit TV of Junior High School Drug Dealers. But Father, as it turns out, is not all that interested in his paternal image; perhaps all we're dealing with here is Mother's own projection of a paternal image.

Father's loss isn't incurred by Mother's entry into the career world, although that gets a bit closer since it changes Mother's position as Father's favorite spectator. While she's out there working, Mother will encounter pretty much the same problems Father does except for the men who want her to sleep with them for the promotion. Working Mother may contribute substantially to Father's loss but it won't simply be because she's working and earning money, and, in any event, Father will most likely shift his romantic strategies to deal with the new situation.

All of these factors, or none of them, may be involved marginally in Father's sense of loss, which he seldom articulates directly to anyone. The loss he feels is an individual loss of identity and personal reference with Mother's feelings as the major measuring device. Essentially it is a lover's loss, from a need fashioned during an earlier time of his life which remains strong during his entire lifetime. While Mother's chances to meet her need for looking after people with love and efficiency bloom with the onset of the family, Father's needs for exclusive possession of his woman are threatened. Being a parent in America is Mother's ballgame and she is everywhere acknowledged as the resident expert on children, as well as the senior authority and critic on fatherhood.

Let's begin the story of Father's odyssey of loss with a consideration of a rock-bottom human need.

The Male Need to Show Off

Inherent in nearly every problem that Father encounters as an adult male and a parent is a most pervasive psychological need: the need to show off. This need is the most vital driving force in the lives of teenaged boys and grown men, and how consistently it is met determines a great deal of their futures as fathers. The chronic, volatile daydreams and fantasies of the young teenaged boy, of conquest and heroism, of accolades and honors, of adulation and death, of winning and the roar of the crowd, simmer and bubble away until a hard core of inner personal necessity is created which is as urgent as hunger and as omnipresent as sex. The need itself can incorporate success, failure, sex, violence and what have you into its internal workings and, on special occasions, can even make dying seem logical.

What is showing off in the male? It is the *performance* of actions before an audience of selected others, especially women, which draws their attention, *plus* an element of admiration, awe or fear which, as we shall see, is not found in garden-variety attention-getting. Next to showing off, attention getting is Father's most powerful motive, especially when dealing with Mother, but the second choice is only tapped for protracted use when all feasible opportunities to show off for her have been foreclosed. Whenever that day arrives it's a sad one for Father, but since his goal is to keep Mother's mind occupied with him, he down-shifts with a minimum of delay.

The experts, naturally, dismiss showing off with a sneer as pathetically immature in those who demonstrate it outright, although they are willing to accord it a place in fantasy and other harmless diversions. Showing off is typically pictured in healthy-living books as a condition indigenous to children and something that all of us must strive to throw off in the name of "growing up," or at least vent into healthy-sounding channels like achievement, productivity, effectiveness and similar inspirationals. Even in books about children this need is mentioned only as a "symptom," either to be mercifully outgrown with time or deliberately dissipated by Dad spending more time with the kid. In short, showing off is officially seen as unhealthy and something that, with any luck at all, we can make go away.

Mother's need to show off is also substantial, but there are two important differences between men and women as they manifest this need. The first difference lies squarely in the performance. Girls not only lack the opportunity to perform but also the background and experience that boys have – even if the latter aren't very successful at it. The real sexual revolution in America will not take place in bedrooms or banks, but on the playing fields of the junior high school, where competitive sports are slowly becoming part of a girl's everyday life. What a few of Father's daughters are learning there even now about competition and violence, cowardice and guts, anger and frustration, amidst the spit and the sweat, will change the marriages of the future more than years of consciousness-raising and couples' encounter groups ever could.

The second sexual difference in showing off is that in Father's version, being liked or loved by the audience is not an essential element of the production, while for Mother it most certainly is. Accordingly, Father is often able to enjoy meeting his need by being the most outrageous, the wildest, the most colorful, the most dangerous, the toughest, or just the baddest dude around in whatever way is relevant to his life. He usually doesn't care all that much about the affections of his watchers; the attention and awe matter more. When Mother shows off, there is always a necessity for a bond of affection and approval between her and her audience, most readily seen with her children, and to be the baddest woman around would only appeal to an occasional eccentric with an unusual background.

Showing off as such is seldom if ever discussed in connection with grown men; instead, a variety of more palatable synonyms are offered for consideration. There are those who write, with varying degrees of fascination, of the male interest in power, which, while sounding slightly sinister, at least implies some type of marginally natural competitiveness. Achievement and ambition are other favorites, especially in the healthy-living books, and it is clear that these terms carry with them some heavy mental-health potential. Prestige and status needs are yet other designations of Father's fuel offered by the more social-minded scholars, but here the implications are a bit shallow and slightly fragile. Finally, the openly castigating expressions of ego-centricity and selfishness are used by those who are sensitive about having been elbowed off the stage more than is fair.

What all of these words miss is the essential performance aspect of showing off and the crucial role of the watcher/admirer. Men show off or attempt to show off in a dizzying variety of ways, many of which in practice are not entirely self-evident, as will be noted shortly. Showing off is even more basic and complex than the term competitive – yet another favorite designation of males. But competitive suggests winning or attempting to win, whereas for the purposes of showing off, if losing will do the job, then losing it will be. The term "potential" is often reserved for just such men who manage to show off by losing, and yet retain the anguished aura of what might have been, especially for those watchers captivated by such challenges.

The modern term "macho" only comes slightly closer. The common grasp of this word suggests that men are not only tougher than women, but that some part of this toughness is fueled by an intense desire not to show weakness. To show weakness is not macho and is to be avoided at all costs, or so it seems. Hardly. Macho simply means overt showing off for a woman, the ultimate showing off. But if weakness does it instead, then weakness it is. This strategy of weakness, which is, of course, never admitted to by the men who employ it, can take a number of different forms. A typical one has Father declaring that the unbearably intense stress at work is taking its toll and might even take him out altogether with cardiac arrest. It all depends on how weakness is marketed, apparently, but weakness it is.

Father's dilemma concerning this need is well illustrated by a review of some of the ways in which men show off on a routine and every-day basis. At the top of the list are those men in professional sports, where the gift of talent is blended as much as possible with the danger and toughness of it all. Thus, racing car drivers, quarterbacks and goalies are watched and admired for their skill and feared for by their fans, lest the cruel fates intervene a bit early. Many scholars see these athletic pursuits as merely violent and self-destructive, which certainly misses the real point that pain is an acceptable price to pay in the service of this need. Generally speaking, when the experts fail to grasp the goal of some behavior, it is labeled self-destructive, partly as an act of rejection of the performer who has chosen to show off so recklessly and illogically. When the performer is a woman, she is called masochistic.

A second style of showing off is found in men who are in different sorts of dangerous occupations; policemen and firemen head the list, but other men often use ingenious means to inject danger into less heroic pursuits. Wearing uniforms and badges helps here, but care must be taken to declare that the men involved selflessly submit to the dangers because they must, and certainly not because it's fun and often exciting. Evening television is a monument to all this, and in case the women are not sufficiently anxious watchers, the police and fire unions nationwide will issue periodic grim reminders of what a terrible and awful burden it all is. Naturally, all of the larger funerals are televised, complete with clanging bands and fervent eulogies for the last defenders of civilization as we know it.

A third major class of performer is defined by the professions of all types, the "status" and "prestige" careers which many mothers aspire to' for their daughters through matrimony. Physicians, dentists, lawyers and the like are in a near chronic state of posturing and posing, showing each new customer who comes through the door just how smart they are. Men who have spent a long time going to school seem to develop a kind of professional welfare mentality that the world owes them something for all that sacrifice. Accordingly, the rules of professional protocol are designed to be clearly intimidating to laymen, just in case. Relying on "image" makes America's professionals a sensitive and touchy bunch. It would all be a lot easier if it were somewhat dangerous as well, and professionals do sometimes take out pistol licenses to supply an added touch of gravity for their intimates.

Another version of showing off is found in men who work in business, corporate or otherwise. This career is perhaps the most difficult of all to mold into a consistently good showing-off performance. Despite all attempts to market themselves as dynamic, two-fisted and hard-hitting, the danger is just not there on its own. The attempted remedy is two-fold: the first solution is to make money the instrument of awe or fear, and Father is sometimes heard to claim incredible coups about large sums of money – either gained or lost, it hardly matters; the second and more common ploy is to make the job itself the potential assassin, whereby the intolerable tension and demands of the work threaten at the age of thirty and up to make Mother a widow. In either case, Father is straining hard to draw some awe, but it's difficult. Either attempt to show off gets tedious, and both are perilously close to simple attention getting, which is second choice precisely because it can't arouse any high-level fire from Mother.

A fifth category of showing off is seen in those men who belong to America's political class. Marketed by themselves and their flacks as "powerful" men, they draw bankers, real-estate men and construction people around them in droves to distribute the public till according to complex schedules of debt and service. The slick urban magazines love this version of showing off, and scarcely a week passes without a breathless insider's report on just why Selectman Monahan double-crossed District Attorney Tortilla by voting against a bill which would have required county deputy sheriffs to leave a tip after a free meal. There are endless restaurant meetings about "deals," and if Mother looks unimpressed, a mention that the Mafia has been seen poking around may bring her to. Indeed, by now the Mafia must number its membership in the millions if we are to believe its frequent use by politicians whenever things get dull. If Father makes it big in the county apparatus, he will quickly strive to get himself a limousine, with chauffeur, or even a bodyguard, much in the manner of black pimps in Times Square, who know a thing or two about showing off. Father will speak somberly of having given his life in "public service" as a "fighter," although it is impossible to tell who the beneficiaries or the enemies are.

What is left for millions of fathers who lack the talent, the danger, the status, or even some contrived power? They are left to improvise their own dramas with whatever is available to use. Some join informal athletic leagues of one type or another, partly for the sheer fun of playing the game and partly to show off for their women, even in a small ballpark. Some fathers become volunteer firemen, desecrate the family car with flashing lights and roar off to each new emergency with stomach a-tingle, hoping that Mother is left behind with at least some small degree of fear and apprehension.

Other fathers become auxiliary policemen and, while the real cops won't let them have guns because they are very jealous about just how many guys are carrying, the element of danger is projected, with some chance of positive results in the watchers. A substantial number of fathers become deeply involved in boys' sports as Little League managers, Pop Warner coaches and instructors of an endless variety. Full of mock morality, they enforce no-cursing rules on the boys, diligently plan the inevitable play-offs and all-star games to keep the season going, and can generally still find time to think of ways to keep girls off the teams. There are many snarling speeches to the little ones about "playing to win," "hard hitting," "when the going gets tough," and like that; frustrated men, now reduced to showing off for ten-year-old boys.

Having a gun around the house is a popular means of showing off for some fathers, and this one has the advantage of invaluable help from many of America's endlessly naive scholars and eternally corruptible politicians of every stripe. Literally scores of both types wail each and every week about the horrors of the violent society America has become because of easy access to firearms. Guns, in fact, have absolutely nothing to do with any of the real violence in the country, the beating and raping of women, the abuse of children and the mugging of the elderly. These victims are selected precisely *because* one does not need a weapon to savage them; one only needs to be a coward. The concept of physical cowardice is a proposition that Father, guilty or not, understands at belt-buckle level right from boyhood, regardless of the diagnoses of the respective cowards' emotional dynamics.

Nor do guns have all that much sexual significance either, despite the fervently hostile explanations of the gun-control advocates that a stiff Smith & Wesson is a replacement, at least in part, for a flaccid and unwilling penis. No, not at all. When one follows the path of 95 percent of the pistols and rifles around, sure enough they end up in close emotional proximity to a woman somewhere along the line. (The other 5 percent are in the possession of professionals of the criminal class or hard-core paranoids looking for their place in the sun, who would not be deterred by any amount of control.) The purpose of it all? To scare Mother, or at least to cause a chronic family problem as to where it should be stored, so the kids shouldn't find it, God forbid. It does the trick, and that's what it's all about. The country's politicians, incidentally, have a very real thing for pistols, and if anyone could ever get an honest count of the licensed carriers, America's dedicated public servants would be high on the list.

Now that the CB radio is in mass distribution, showing off has been made possible for some fathers who may have been deprived for some time. Their sadly urgent messages of "Breaker, Breaker" (Here I am, guys) are delivered with a real-guy gusto that captures a tiny bit of roles and images long gone by. To top off a day, perhaps some playfully aggressive lines to a few little beavers out there who are also showing off can bring feelings of substance and satisfaction not easily gained elsewhere.

And where ingenuity of this type fails, and the deeds and performances are just not possible, then words alone will have to do: Father *lies* a lot about the circumstances of his life, both past and present. The male capacity to lie is always underestimated and, when acknowledged at all, is simply put off as bragging or boasting, which misses the essential point that many of the boasts are factually false from the beginning. There is something of an unwritten code among men that no one will be called for a few lies unless he really goes too far. Thus, when a man is openly regarded as a "bullshit artist" by his peers, it is clear that he is a consistent violator of the gentlemen's agreement.

As a young wife Mother sometimes catches onto the lying but tries mightily to put it out of her mind because to reflect on its meaning is too disturbing. The lies Father tells Mother, and sometimes the kids, represent deliberate distortions of the facts for showing-off purposes. The lies can be about anything at all, but tend to concentrate on spectacular, dangerous or gutsy deeds, yesterday or today, or, in head-to-head competition with the children, how much tougher it all was when Dad was a child.

When Mother shows off she seldom seems to have any need to lie about herself and her life. The lies she does tell about herself, her children, how she spends money and the like, are more often told to conserve and conceal than to capture center stage. Simply to be married is showing off, and being a mother is an even larger showing-off enterprise. While there is much current discourse about alternative life styles for women, having a child still puts Mother even-up with the other girls where it counts. Mother often shows off the place she lives in, both inside and out, but here the values expressed are beauty and taste, qualities far removed from danger, fear or awe. Mother will sometimes show off her body, but this expression is not nearly as intense or as blatantly sexual as men sometimes think or wish it to be.

Showing off for the kids is Mother's biggest admiration-generator, and the advantage here is that it can often be done without anyone being the wiser. Under any circumstances, children are connected to their mother by high-voltage wires, and these make them perfect audiences for Mother to demonstrate her wisdom, compassion and general grasp of life. Indeed, a fair proportion of what children hear as criticism directed at them is not that at all, it is Mother (or Father) showing off by proving to the kids how smart they are.

For most fathers, showing off eventually fails because of age, lack of any real talent, or simply because it just can't be expedited very successfully with the kids around. Little by little for most, very quickly for some, the need to show off is frustrated, and even lying doesn't improve Father's position all that consistently. Father's rage begins to build, and he starts to act with a simpler, but equally dedicated motive. Meanwhile Mother, with her need to show off better met by marriage and parenthood, settles more consistently into her own motivational style, which she hopes will bring her the kinds of rewards she seeks. As Mother and Father face each other as spouses and lovers, their most pressing needs are often going in savagely different directions.

To appreciate attention getting and its essential components, it is necessary to visit briefly with another woman in Father's life, his mother. All but a few of us were raised by women, and the effects of this don't rub off. They are different for boys than for girls, and the long-range consequences for men and women are powerful and far-reaching. For the background of attention getting, Father's second most intense need in dealing with Mother in particular, let's return to the early teenage years, where the action is.

Love's Prototype: Mother and Teenage Son

Watching just about any mother in her daily dealings with her teenaged son provides a panoramic view of the essentials of the love relationship which will occur years later in the grown man's life. The Mother-Sonny connection flashes with passion and intensity, rage and affection, tenderness and hostility, and need and anxiety on both sides. If it's involvement one is looking for, here it is. Things really start cooking when the boy is in the age range of eleven to thirteen, a time of maximum change in the child's life. It is important to note too that Mother is typically zealous and energetic about her son, so that she too is all primed to play her part in the drama about to unfold.

The twelve-year-old boy is at an age when management and control of him are getting difficult. His manner and temper are changing quite independently of anything going on at home. His style suddenly becomes surlier and dramatically less verbal when dealing with his parents. He is prone now to being secretive and often seems entirely distracted; for the first time, Sonny is now described as moody.

Then there's the physical thing. He is getting bigger and stronger and very absorbed in measuring just how strong he is in comparison with the other guys. He is also developing sexually and masturbation is threatening to become his life's calling. Control of the boy's behavior, therefore, moves on to some awfully shaky ground. And if physical discipline has been a major element of control during the earlier years, the family ship is already in heavy seas.

The mental-health books describe this period as the beginning of the growing child's surge for independence. Mother is solemnly counseled as to the proper schedule to follow in granting her child his gradual emancipation. But the power to grant *anything* is precisely what is now at issue. The boy himself is in a terrible bind. He loves his mother and needs her just as before, but now he is often hateful and angry in addition. He is into the peer world now and is beginning to measure himself against different rules. He still looks for her and hates himself for doing so. Boys are easily embarrassed by their mothers at this age, and the development of their own sexuality is only a part of it.

The big source of anguished conflict is really his desire not to be a baby any more, but, of course, his need to be her baby is intense. Mother, however, sees his withdrawal from her as a sign of rejection and disapproval, signaling the approach of a time that truly threatens and frightens her. Mother knows that, unlike her daughter whom she confidently expects to have around her in one way or another, for the rest of her days, this child will someday go away with another woman and will not return unless struck by total disaster. And that other woman, Mother also realizes, not only comes equipped with her own mother, but will not take kindly to any excessive display of interest in Sonny under any conditions.

Imagine for a moment all the services and value that Mother provides for Sonny. She cooks for him and feeds him. She keeps his clothing clean and mended and buys any new clothes for him, lest he select in poor taste or value. She picks up after him and tends to his needs lovingly. She *does* for him. And when he chooses to talk, he shows off for Mother, who is indeed the most receptive of audiences, as he recounts his feats of derring-do or recites his latest outrages on the world; these tales, true or not, leave Mother admiring or aghast as the case may be. She also hounds and harasses him, nags him unmercifully, shouts and screams at him, as he does to her, says vicious and hurtful things to him, as he does to her, but more than anything else, she *talks* to him. Physically, at least, the two parties are best pictured with Mother engaged in a monologue about one terribly important aspect of his life or another, and Sonny, slumped usually, silent and surly, mooning off toward some vague and distant horizon.

But through it all, both service and storms, she is paying attention to him. She is setting a precedent as to the level of attention that will someday be the bench-mark by which he assesses the amount of "love" he receives from another woman. And because the boy is still literally looking up at her, his mother is clearly the strongest, most powerful, most perceptive, most aggressive, most sensitive, most loving woman in the world. Mother, for her part, her own needs sizzling audibly, never tires of reinforcing that impression in his mind.

When the Mother-Sonny flight takes off, the kind of exchanges they have in anger and frustration would do justice to the world's most intense adult lovers. There is ploy and counter-ploy, threat and counter-threat, silence and counter-silence. There are substantial numbers of teenaged boys who can't seem to recall talking to their mothers at all except in anger. From his point of view the issue, as usual, is control, and from hers, her fear of rejection. Mother puts it differently, of course: bad habits of an endless variety; cleanliness sometimes; unwholesome companions often; late hours occasionally; school performance and behavior are always legitimate; respect is a big one; vulgar and profane language, a maturational essential for boys, is also high on the list; and, of course, if all else fails, the threat of drugs and alcohol. But do they love each other? Oh, yes, they love each other, and they need each other.

In most of these mother-son connections an aura of motivated deliberateness grows unmistakeably between the two partners. Mother is often heard to remark that Sonny has committed some especially devious sin "on purpose," and she is right. As the struggle for control rolls on, she demands, he withholds; she reminds, he forgets; she is competent, he is a fool; she is articulate, he mumbles; she is spiteful, he is wounded; she is conciliatory, he is vicious. And through it all she is bragging to her friends about him or bitterly complaining to them, which serves the same purpose. If the amounts of attention and agitated involvement are the measuring rods of a love relationship, this one is at the top of the heap.

Now if there is one thing that zealous Mother cannot tolerate from her child (this is even far truer with daughters), it is the child's unwillingness to "tell her everything" that he is thinking, everything that happens in his life, and every emotional twinge in his viscera. Thus, the big trouble between the two lovers begins over talking, or rather the son's reluctance to do so. Mother's intense need for the boy to talk to her and his crafty and sullen withholding of speech take on powerful significance at a later time in the boy's life, when he will be living with a different woman. It is primarily around this theme that diligent Mother also demonstrates two vital skills of great future import.

She *pursues* him. She literally and physically pursues him. To appreciate this extraordinary psychology of space, imagine the following common scene: Sonny returns from school, and Mother says, "Hello there." He grunts and continues on to his own place. Within fifteen seconds she will be there, right there, physically next to him. "What's the matter with you? I said 'Hello' to you, and you treat me like I wasn't there." Sonny grunts again and says, "Nothing's the matter." But Mother persists. "Don't tell me that – I see it all over your face." Young teenager mumbles again, "Nothing's the matter. Nothing is bothering me." While this therapeutic attack is irritating to him, there is something comforting about it as well. Deep in his heart he feels soothed by Mother's belief that if there is anything wrong in his life, it is her sacred pledge to him to set it right, even against his will.

Nothing deters her. "I know you are not being honest. You are not telling me everything. What happened at school today? I know something happened, didn't it?" Sonny replies, now with a mounting mix of anger, exasperation and relief, "Nothing happened at school or anywhere else." But Mother closes in, firing one hypothesis after another in order of probability, and usually it doesn't take her long to strike paydirt. Sonny looks up at her quickly, with eyes momentarily widened, yet still evasive, and it's all right there: *she knows.* And that reveals the second special talent that Mother shows Sonny.

She reads his mind. She actually reads his mind, and he knows it. Children never understand that "reading their minds" is not all that difficult, because the events of their lives are reasonably visible to any adult watching closely. Be that as it may, Sonny is very impressed, as he has always been. Indeed, the tension of the emotional situation is now released by Mother's mind-reading and, sure enough, moments later they are chatting and buzzing, with Mother, of course, doing most of the talking, but with Sonny at least animated and participating. The combination of Mother's persistent pursuit and Sonny's unwillingness to talk about his troubles has produced another in a long line of successful mind-readings and another effective solution to the boy's problem.

The love affair between Mother and Sonny has been reviewed because many of his future difficulties as a father have been established there. He has received a dizzying level of attention, however conflicted, which will help years later to make him fragile and vulnerable to competitors, especially his own children. Many of his basic attitudes and expectations about women and the way in which he expresses his most fundamental feelings have also been established here. These bittersweet fruits blossom years later when Father is living with another woman nearer his own age; Father did not marry his mother, or did he?

With Mother and Sonny as necessary background, let's return again to the motives of Father as a grown man and Mother as a grown woman.

Women: Approval Seekers/Men: Attention Getters

Girls are still raised to be socially responsive creatures with a flair for getting adult persons to respond to them affirmatively and positively. They need people to say, "That's a good girl; that's a good job." "You are doing well." "You look nice." People who are strongly motivated to seek approval ask a lot of questions because that's the safest and easiest way to make sure that approval is forthcoming. They generally don't volunteer answers, they don't make decisions, and they stay on the right side of those powerful other people who do, and who give approval.

Women who have not achieved insight into this motive often say they seek only "appreciation," apparently to imply that the key element sought is simply a civilized response to good service, rather than an acknowledgment of the dependencies and anxieties which lie at a more basic level. They do not understand why they have tended to gravitate to apparently strong individuals. Many young wives put it this way: "He always seemed so decisive and strong to me before we were married." Showing off usually works at that age.

It would seem that this is literally what is meant by people who say they want someone to look up to, in the vertical, approval-seeking way. But look up to for what? What the young wife often discovers is that there is nobody up there after all, at least for what she needs to find. Her new husband is intent on gratifying his own needs, which have little to do with being looked up to in the way she means, or at best are conflicted around this point.

Approval-seeking people are virtuous people, good people. They want to be, and they have to be. Like the classic girl-child the feminist movement rails so vehemently against, she is trained to be good and nice, to show caring and softness, to do whatever it takes to make people pat her on the head. It is partly this element that gives the "beauty and the beast" flavor to so many marriages, with the mother, publicly at least, showing all the social niceties, knowing what to do, what to say and when to say it, and the father quiet, sometimes rude, and generally distant and distracted, except for those few men showing off at the time.

It is far more than the cultural stereotypes of female upbringing, however, which makes most girls into approval seekers. Children as always are very smart, and little girls learn all on their own that they are physically the weakest and most vulnerable of all human types around. A young girl is afraid of her father, for instance, even if he never hits her and is the gentlest of men, simply because she knows where she stands physically should a fight ever occur. To avoid violence becomes a matter of high priority to her, and while the adult world around her prattles on about how cute she is and similar claptrap, little Sis is staying out of harm's way by the means she knows best, which do not include the reckless alternative of punching somebody in the mouth. Years later she may be a rape victim and, ironically, her childhood apprehensions and confusions turn out to be correct. She now has to demonstrate to judges, lawyers and cops, at least for respect if not for a conviction, that she put up a hell of a fist fight before having her legs spread. If, on the other hand, she takes a beating or two from her husband without blowing the whistle on him, then of course she's clearly masochistic. Ah, the experts!

Approval seekers become immersed in order, form and neatness, because they are so terribly vulnerable to criticism, not merely of themselves, but of everything around them. Everything has to be just right; everything has to be in its place. She must be ever alert so that some small detail casually passed by will not rise to haunt her with the threat of disapproval. As a mother, her preoccupation with order matures into a need to "balance" everything properly, which exposes her to a circle of criticism and causes endless problems with Father.

Remote and distant people who are stingy with compliments and applause make approval seekers anxious and nervous. The result is that they have to try ever so much harder for these people. They have to share and give, smile and perform, work and endure, as a constant plea to be looked upon favorably. When the prized approval giver criticizes instead, the girl says she is "hurt," partly because she has worked so hard for the reward that didn't materialize, and partly because she is unable to verbalize that she is angry enough to kill.

To be "hurt" itself seems the logical feeling for approval seekers who believe that rewards of all kinds should be reachable by honest effort and endurance, rather than by violent or devious means. At any point along the way, hurt carries with it the seeds of Mother's final ace in her love-match war with Father: martyrdom, one of Mother's staples for showing off. She has worked so terribly hard and given so much of herself to a surly and unappreciative man, with no results of any direct use to her, that at least she can claim that no other woman has suffered and endured quite as much as she has. This pose not only trumps Father's sulking behavior, but redefines it for the children so that years later they still wonder, "how she ever took it for so long."

Approval-seeking people commonly misread their own negative feelings. They are so used to searching the world for the "right" response, the winning behavior, the acts or words that will make others say, "That's good," that their own feelings inevitably become confused. Anger out in the open does not make people say that someone is nice and good. Anger out in the open also runs the considerable risk of making stronger people angry in return, which brings the fear again, or worse. Assertiveness training, one of the current palliatives for timidity, carefully restricts its lessons to harmless environments and safe people. The professional trainers, themselves showing off their fearlessness in perfect safety, never venture near the fear, the bottom line of approval seeking.

Approval seekers are often gullible. Since approval seeking depends so heavily on words and talking, approval seekers are tempted to believe anything that any potential approval giver says to them. They hear the words, take them literally, and try to modify their behavior accordingly. When Mother calls for an honest and open (and verbal) relationship, it's her plea to be told the rules of the exchange and the kinds of approval to expect and strive for. "Tell me what it is you want. Tell me what you need." Relationships which are not honest and open in her eyes are merely "playing games" and are a source of deep and genuine frustration for her. Considered a bit differently, approval seekers are often in the position of extracting promises from others because hearing the right words has acquired a high value of its own, even when the promises are not kept and the same promises must be solicited anew a little later.

Finally, since approval seeking is a need inherently defined by "happy endings," Mother is often entirely at cross-purposes in life with Father, who avoids happy endings as if they were cancer. To Mother, a happy ending means relief from the anxiety of disapproval and loneliness, and a sign that life is back in balance again, with the danger past. It appears to her that this is a state of affairs obviously worth maintaining. This is apparently not so in Father's scheme of things, since he always seems to find something to knock the balance out of whack. Most couples have an awful time "getting it together" for very long before some kind of trouble breaks out, and the whole struggle starts over again. To understand Father's contribution, the motive called attention getting, that need which surfaces when the opportunities to show off have dried up or become sporadic and ineffective, must be examined.

Most of what current professionals say about showing off as a need can be applied to attention getting without modification: it is childish, immature, and is to be discouraged and frowned upon by all right thinkers. While attention getting does not produce the admiration or fear that successful showing off does, it adds an element which showing off does not feature: it is *disruptive*. Attention getters disturb others, interrupt otherwise harmonious proceedings and destroy feelings of well-being around them.

Hard-core attention getters are volatile and not nearly as manageable as approval seekers generally are. It is a truly selfish motive as well, since there is seldom any social benefit or service to others in the process, as there usually is in approval seeking.

Just what is attention getting? It's getting the pivotal person in his life *involved* with him in *any way* whatever, by *any means* that it takes, and *keeping* her that way, happily or angrily, it makes no difference. To hell with admiration and awe. That is the part that Mother finds difficult to understand. Because her own needs have her deeply committed to balance and happy endings, it makes no sense to her that Father is not also oriented to the final relief of approval. It's true, of course, that one can be good and get the approval version of attention, but being disruptive really brings people close, does it quicker, and keeps them longer. There are no values involved in attention getting. If telling the truth does it that's fine; if not, then toss in a lie or two. Attention getting seems insatiable, without beginning or end, and happy endings can only be tolerated infrequently, because to fathers they mean the end of attention.

How does Father go about doing it? One favorite method is seeking sympathy with health complaints, because it challenges the sensitive side of Mother and makes her worry about him. This is not ordinary hypochondriasis, which Mother herself is more versatile at, with its legion of chronic and undramatic complaints; this is heart-attack country. Business executives and professionals have this one honed to a glistening edge. Not a month passes when the male media do not proudly trumpet the latest dire findings on that Valhalla of attention getting: the executive cardiac syndrome. So, while the mean life expectancy continues to soar closer to senility, Father, with a straight face, reminds her constantly that he could go at any time. Just how many of the millions of heart conditions are legit is anybody's guess, but they keep Mother concerned and worried lest the stress of his job take him out prematurely. Worry – that's attention.

Staying away from home is a big one too, because most men live with a woman who wants to know where he is and usually wants him at home. There are even women who will stay up to wait for him, to shout and scream and harangue him for his devious and hurtful ways. This will be true sometimes even when he has presumably been working late at his job. Anger – that's attention.

Sleeping is also effective because it not only frustrates, upsets and depresses her that he is not even interested in her and the kids enough to keep awake, but it is also useful to suggest a serious fatigue problem, perhaps overwork. Upsetting her – that's attention.

Moderate alcoholism is also popular with men, because it implies that he's got some dark problem that Mother can only guess at. She will be frightened as to what it might mean. Some fathers achieve the same result by driving the car wildly, until Mother is near hysteria from fear. Scaring her – that's attention.

Implying to her that he's *not really happy* in a manner to be discussed shortly is the major technique of attention getters. It strikes at the very heart of approval seekers because it suggests the final failure and the ultimate disapproval. The unhappiness is seldom verbalized, because it is seldom really true. But, no matter, the look of it is sufficient. It frustrates her need for a happy ending, and it depresses her. Depressing her – that's attention.

Now all of these words – anger, worry, depression, upset, nervousness, frustration, scared – are not only on the grim and negative side, but are also a far cry from Mother's understanding of giving attention, which is to look at someone and listen to him talk. What do they all have in common? They are all obsessive words, meaning that she is thinking about him, her mind is occupied with him. She is worrying, angry, depressed, upset, nervous, frustrated and frightened, just like his mother was. The final goal of Father's attention getting is to have Mother *obsess about him,* just as his mother did, and just as he does about her; to think of him constantly all day long, as he does of her; not talking, but thinking, obsessing.

Are there good times and happy endings? Of course there are.

But Father often has only token faith in that style, because when Mother is feeling good she moves away from him and starts balancing things again, which inevitably means less obsession with him. Obsessing is the true male measure of love, and just as men apply it to their own feelings, so they apply it to women. To get attention is to be noticed and obsessed about, and to be obsessed about is to be loved. If he feels that her mind is wandering from him, he will do or say anything, relevant or irrelevant, to disrupt the proceedings and to regain her concentration, however anguished.

Attention getting is also an inherently competitive motive, and it is important to understand what competitiveness here means. It has nothing to do with other men directly, nor is it at all related to the naive notions of male dominance or superiority over women, which seem to fascinate certain writers. It has to do with obsessional competition. Father is jealous of and competitive with any idea, person, event, sensation, feeling, twinge, job, family, child, abstraction, and even pain that might be occupying Mother's mind, thereby indicating that he is not. The purpose of attention getting, therefore, is to drive away every such thought from her mind by whatever means are at his disposal – to capture her mind.

This is the major reason why Father almost never tells the truth when Mother asks what it was she did to make him angry and to change his mood so suddenly. He is slightly embarrassed and even guilty. He feels that if he ever did tell her that he is angry because she looked a bit too happy frolicking with their son, because she concentrated a bit too intensely on their daughter's latest tale, because she seemed actually to enjoy a late night out with her girlfriends, or because she stayed up late relishing a good book, that she would laugh incredulously and think him quite mad. At the very least she would think him childish. The attention-getting, competitive male is always only a step away from rage about what is apparently going on in her head.

And, finally, attention getters have an incredible eye and ear for physical detail of a certain type. It's not the approval seeker's flair for order and neatness, nothing like that at all; it's a grasp of his quarry's physical whereabouts and location. *Where* Mother is is paramount; whom she is with is important but less so. Many fathers have developed the persistent habit of calling Mother during the work day. She usually believes the purpose of these calls is simply to transmit domestic information or to trade affectionate banalities. Far from it. Father is tracking her every move, and the calls resemble the "checking" that anxious pre-schoolers do to see if Mommy is still there. He wants to know where she is, what she's doing, and with whom.

The answers will usually determine his mood when next he sees her. If he calls and she's not there, his first question later is, "Where were you?" If she asks, "Does it matter?" his answer, of course, is "No." When it is Father who starts asking questions, he is edging close to fear and trying hard to conceal it from Mother, lest she see through it and realize the dependent position the questioner is always in. But she accepts his denial as a matter of course, indicating his apparent lack of interest and confirming some feelings she has had for some time now. After all, why would anyone lie about anything so simple?

Do fathers seek approval too? Often from the children, but that's another story. Some do from Mother. They are called "weak" by Mother and later by the children as well. In such cases, Mother is labeled "castrating" by the male establishment to cover the embarrassment of Father's willing surrender and obvious happiness in his role with Big Mama. Is Mother ever a show-off and attention getter in Father's style? Sometimes, but rarely. In this case, Father is worse than "weak"; he is the one about whom everyone asks, "How does he put up with her?" Attention-getting girls are a different order altogether because they terrify everybody, and in their frequent scrapes with the Family Court they arouse a rare kind of wrath from the virtuous bureaucrats idling about.

While Father has been consoling himself at the loss of showing-off opportunities by perfecting the techniques of keeping Mother frustrated and upset so as to gain her attention, she, on her part, has become pretty dissatisfied and bored. She often concludes that the man she has committed herself to does not love her.

The Male Language of Love: Anger and Silence

But the man she got really does love her – he does indeed. And he needs her – he needs her almost unbearably. But Mother and Father are having severe and chronic difficulties – which are not created by the presence of the kids, but merely exacerbated by them – difficulties about the meaning of loving. Mother, who is always balancing things, says to Father, "I need you as my friend and husband, as my companion and my lover, as the father of my children, as the man who completes my life. I need you to *fit in*." Father, who is always obsessing, says to Mother, "I need you," period. Father's need for her is so much narrower and so dramatically less specific, it is small wonder that their language of love is so different.

For Mother, loving is generally a fairly straightforward proposition, largely based, as has been said, on the approval-seeking model. If you love someone, you *do* for him. You *show* him that you love him. You show him that you care. You show him that you want his approval, and that loving is a wonderful condition to be in. For Mother, loving is a matter of zeal and enthusiasm. Love is a matter of sharing and always trying to be nice to each other. It all sounds so healthy and wholesome, surely it must mean the same to Father.

Wrong! For Father, loving is a matter of involvement, and very little else. What's involvement? Attention and obsession, of course, spending most of your waking moments thinking about the loved one, either with affection or anger. To obsess is everything; to be unable to drive that person out of your mind. Whether such involvement makes anybody feel better doesn't seem to matter in the slightest. Happy endings are all right periodically, but they are quite irrelevant to involvement. The attention and possession of Mother is the objective.

What is it, then, that seems to have Father so angry? It is more than just the mourning for his waning capabilities to show off for her. It's really the frustration of his possessive and attention-getting needs by Mother's capacity to balance loving him along with several other people who matter greatly to her. As Mother often feels entirely unloved and unappreciated because she misreads the male expression, so Father usually feels that she doesn't love him enough amidst all the balancing. Therefore, of course, he is almost constantly angry. That's the pair of them: Mother often feeling that she is not loved *at all*, and Father feeling that he's not loved *enough*; Mother disappointed, hurt and bored, Father angry and silent.

Mother sometimes gets a glimmer of what's going on behind his pose, but she usually rationalizes it away by thinking that he only *needs* her, but that he doesn't really *want* her. This nice distinction is the approval seeker's way of saying that everyone should want to please others as she does and other mature people do; needing someone is for children. The word "need" is additionally ugly because it implies that any woman at all could fulfill it – another approval loser.

As always, there isn't much help for them from today's Love Doctors. Without fail, the emotion experts turn a contemptuous eye on relationships based on "mere dependency." Such connections, in their view, are clearly second-level stuff, falling far short of what a "real" relationship is all about. There is, after all, so much more to loving than the simple recognition of mutual needing and sexual chemistry, they say. That simple stuff may be O.K. for the psychological riff-raff, but for sensitive and aware people, love in its purer and more divine forms can only be had where Mother and Father are open, trusting, vulnerable, fragile and just so goddamned cute that it makes you cry watching them.

To make matters worse, Father's anger is seriously and continuously underestimated by Mother and the professionals alike. He really *is* mad, at least when he's at home. The fact that his anger is misread only makes him angrier. The combination of his discounted anger and the misperception of his competitiveness about Mother reaches its apex in professional writings on the arrival of the first child. More will be said about this later, but it must be noted here that the tone of these advisers tends to be terribly ootsy poo. They usually say something like, "Now listen, girls, be a teeny bit careful here. Our new Daddy may be a tiny bit jealous of that beautiful little bundle who is coming, so try to do a little something extra for him every week." Having touched that base, the advisers complete their exercise of missing the point by letting Mother know that if new Father behaves erratically, it probably means that he's an immature punk who is just terrified by all that responsibility. The maturity propagandist is addicted to sophisticated "interpretations" of the obvious. What actually goes on at that time is known to many, but spoken of by few, and it has nothing whatever to do with responsibility. The reason for all the fury is straightforward jealousy.

These differences about the meaning of love reach fruition in the significance to the two lovers of *talking*. Mother believes in talking, while Father does not, or at least not in the same way. Mother in her zeal believes that when there is a problem in the relationship, it should be talked out and the solution uncovered. As we shall see, Father only believes in this when Mother is sizing up another man for possibly serious purposes; in all other cases, Father doesn't believe in it at all.

What is called marriage counseling provides an excellent illustration of this difference. Marriage counseling is primarily predicated on a verbal premise: we are here to talk out our problems. In the usual situation it is Mother who comes with the problem that the marriage has reached very difficult times. She sits forward on the edge of her chair, eyes fixed on the counselor, full of tension about the crisis, and describes the events leading up to the present condition, always featuring the complaint of not enough talking. Father, on the other hand, sits back in his chair, his eyes flitting about the room, sizing up the place, obviously uncomfortable in the situation, and clearly threatened by the idea that somebody is going to delve into his connection with Mother.

Father comes most reluctantly and will find numerous reasons for not coming at all. He will often set new records for non-verbal behavior in the counselor's office, and the few answers Father does make are enough to shake the counselor's self-confidence for the evening. No, he says, there is nothing wrong with the relationship that he can see, and, No, he isn't really sure why Mother feels the way she does, and, Yes, he loves the children, and he can't see how they might be connected to all this, and, No, come to think of it, he doesn't know why he's here in the first place – because he really doesn't have any big problems.

Mother corrects him. Of course you're unhappy, she says, or at least you always look like you are. And there's just no communication at all between us, she says, as she has been telling him for the past ten or fifteen years, with the same basic script repeated over and over again. Father concedes that he's unhappy about his job, of course, but that's about the extent of it. But Mother keeps coming back at him, trying to convince him that there can be a better life for them, and he continues to sit and listen. The counselor, his own needs for a happy ending churning consciously, is perplexed and begins to formulate some preliminary diagnoses of Father.

What Mother finds hard to accept is that Father *is* satisfied with the life they have, just the way it is, or pretty nearly so. Yes, he's rip-roaring mad a good part of the time, but he has her, or at least he's living within the same space, and that is what he wants. Father is bound and determined to keep her there as well, and this requires his constant care to keep just far enough away from her to keep her coming at him, just as she's doing now. He obsesses about her nearly all the time, so he's aware that he truly loves her. Could the marriage be improved? Oh, sure, but Father, as noted earlier, has a fair idea of what that means and he's not having any *less* of her attention than he has now. Father's best move, therefore, is to deny that anything very important is wrong, while still maintaining the look of disaster to keep Mother pursuing him. He is, of course, scolded by Mother and counselor alike for being a closed person.

Mother reports, for example, that on a recent evening Father asked her to sit down with him in the family room. Ah, sighs Mother, perhaps a thaw is in the air, and a burst of harmony is just around the corner. But no sooner had Mother sat down than Father turned on the television. To Mother, sitting down together still means that there should be a talk, and she wonders to herself what he wanted her there for. If she reads, that's merely irritating to him, since she's still sitting there with him. If she gets up to make or receive a phone call, that jars him, but he is soothed when she returns. Then Mother gets jumpy – nothing is happening. She is just sitting there, half watching the stupid TV show with him.

Finally, she gets up and goes to the kitchen to *do* something, and he, of course, is now sitting in a silent rage. Later that evening he may comment caustically on the sag in her belly, or tomorrow morning he may "forget" to kiss her good-bye in retaliation. What Father wanted from her was to have her sitting there with him – physically with him. That is Father's rendition of the verb *to possess*: to have her physically there, regardless of what's going on. Depending on one's point of view, this need might be seen as sweet and romantic, or as stupid and childish. Mother often doesn't see it at all, and that makes for some terribly ineffective living.

To replay the scene above for what it means to Father, it is necessary to get Mother's appraisal of it. She often says, "He doesn't really notice anything. Nothing, absolutely nothing. Put on that TV or put him behind a newspaper, and the house could burn down around him. He'd never notice – he's completely unconscious." Nothing could be farther from the truth. Father's keen and obsessive eye for physical detail had Mother's doings covered every second of the evening. Father knows whom she spoke to on the phone, what she read and what she did when she left the room. That's Father's version of involvement. What's the catch, then, if he's so absorbed in her? Well, in the first place, this kind of involvement does little if anything for Mother's needs. And secondly, even if it did, Father will not admit it anyway. Asking Father to own up to any aspect of his tracking of her leads generally to a bald-faced *No*.

It is the consistency of this behaviour which, in part, fuels the popular belief that men are extremely closed about their feelings because they were deliberately taught as little boys not to express their emotions. That was for girls. The belief continues that boys are trained to hide their feelings and are encouraged to model what little boys think of as big, strong men, as in "strong, silent type." The naive assumptions are always made that boys and girls have the very same feelings to express, and, of course, that the market for expression would be the same for both sexes.

To believe this notion, which currently creates unlimited confusion in "couples communication," one must see men as absurdly passive creatures, total victims of their early training as to the meaning of masculinity, poor dumb brutes who are at the mercy of some terribly restrictive social views about sexuality. The "cure" for Father, naturally, is for him to "expose his feelings," "accept his emotional vulnerability," "to take risks," and all those breathless bromides the self-help seminars peddle in profusion.

The "open mouth" theory of communication misses the heart of the matter with a vengeance. It misses the intense motivation of men, it misses their extraordinary sense of space, and it misses the deliberateness that Mother observes so readily in her teen-aged Sonny. Silence is, like lying, a dramatically motivated state in men, and their awareness level is far higher than current opinions seem inclined to credit them with. Their play-acting has worked, and they seem to have everybody fooled.

Father always says *No*. He always denies the extent of his obsession. It's a deliberate lie that Father tells, with the probable objective of keeping whatever position of strength he has with Mother. The lie helps to conceal the need in him, which, during times of real crisis for him, is often so terrifyingly intense that Father is on the verge of becoming unglued altogether.

The denial does other things as well. That he stays silent allows him to test just how concerned she is with him. Father's silence says, "If you really loved me, you wouldn't have to ask." It's mind reading he's after, of course, but it is even more than that. As noted earlier, being verbally fluent about his feelings only makes life easier for Mother, and in fact will lose her interest and attention rather than gain it. If talking means that the "problem," whatever it may be, will be resolved, sure enough her mind begins to wander again, and she's happily back to balancing her many emotional equities. Father fears settling the problem because through the settlement immediately wafts the disturbing scent of insignificance.

Nor will Father admit to the anger. That too would be reckless. He continues to challenge Mother's perceptions of eye and ear, and Mother lives for long stretches of time genuinely confused. Father looks and acts like somebody with a mad on, and yet her continual inquiries produce equally persistent denials. Again, Father's meaning is that if she were paying attention she would know very well that he was angry, and if she really loved him completely she would even know why. Partly as a consequence of the need for mind reading, men have developed an interesting set of code words to express anger: *bored*, *busy* and *tired* are the most common, but numerous others appear in special circumstances.

Well, does all of this mean that Father loves Mother? Precisely. But it also means that his love is often not very functional for her, partly because it's not designed to be, and partly because Mother's needs are frequently in opposite directions. Father has neither plan nor purpose for possessing her. It is just to possess her, that she be there. His need is simply to keep her to himself, to maintain the attention level that her natural approval-seeking pursuit of him has helped to produce, never to admit how much obsessive attention he pays to her comings and goings, and, above all, to maintain whatever singular importance he has to her, even if that only means that he can make her crazier and angrier than anyone else in the world.

The Long Sulk

There is no way of knowing at precisely what moment Father decides that he's not going to get from Mother what he needs. The arrival of this moment is partly determined by how well Father is meeting his need to show off for her naturally. Mother's ability to see through his act and to read him more realistically is another major factor in this development. By the time family living has landed on Father, he is in serious difficulty if Mother does even the minimum necessary amount of sharing and balancing. Father has by this time recognized that however Mother feels about him, she does indeed have other things on her mind. Father's final solution to the entire dilemma is the long sulk.

What is sulking? While obviously a derivative of the childhood temper tantrum, sulking is a skill that men have developed and crafted into a true wonder of human behavior. Sulking is the ability to be angry and to make sure everyone is aware of it and, of course, it requires absolute silence. To an inquiry as to what the trouble might be, a simple "nothing" is sufficient response. Sulking must also convey a certain timeless quality, and in addition it must be ignited by something that only the most diligent observer might recognize. Is the sulk deliberate and especially reserved for Mother? Of course. It is a measured and motivated male expression of feelings. Is Father really angry? At that moment he is.

Compare sulking to pouting, which is Mother's specialty. Is she angry? Yes, but she can still talk, and the posture of the pout implies there's a temporariness and the possibility of healing. If Father cares to inquire what's wrong, even though he usually knows, Mother will tell him without too much effort. The pout is often accompanied by tears, which are a kind of crisis plea to make up and to set things right again. Implicit in pouting is the prospect of a happy ending.

There are several varieties of sulker. There is the "weak"

father mentioned earlier who is quickly brought to heel by a counter-sulk from Mother. Ignoring the sulk with one of her own is strong medicine for Father, and before long he is trying to find an acceptable reason to abandon the sulk and gain her approval. The more common sulker, however, is more professional by far because he is not afraid to sulk in public, the nemesis of all approval seekers. Finally, the superstars of sulking go literally to their graves or to nursing homes with it, apparently enjoying their last grim triumph of painful proof that she didn't love him enough after all.

Is there any effective antidote to the long sulk that a sincere approval seeker might use? Well, there are a couple. A tough counter-sulk from Mother will often do the job, except that it puts Mother in a bad position for her own needs. Mind reading will also do it. But Mother often has trouble seeing the motivational intensity behind Father's sulk that she senses so quickly in her son. Approval seekers see all this as a failure of *doing*, rather than *thinking*, so that they tend to become absorbed in examining their behaviour to see what they did wrong. Mother is generally still pretty sincere about wanting to please Father, not realizing that he doesn't care all that much about being pleased, as long as she is obsessing about him.

But the motivation for the sulk is there to see. All the deliberateness, all the goal-directedness, all the signs which show how much effort, concentration and deviousness are being put into it can be *seen*, but seldom *heard*, because Father is not talking. "Well," Mother sometimes says once she sees through it all, "who wants to live like this? Why should I have to be his mother and read his mind?" And she's right, of course. If it could all be done with words, married living would be a good deal more efficient and easier, which is exactly what Father is intent on preventing.

One major objective of Father's long sulk is to punish Mother by withholding what he really knows she wants, various forms of his participation, some talking, and, of course, his approval. Withholding is the motivated part. Withholding is the natural consequence of the long sulk, and most fathers become expert at it. Whatever Father withholds is custom tailored to fit Mother, although Father's philosophy to support the withholding often seems to fluctuate with the winds. If Mother is tight-fisted about money, then Father develops tendencies to be a sport which make her anxious and upset. If Mother is the more generous one, then Father launches into conservative speeches about the value of money. If Mother is the social one, as she usually is, Father is a real stay-at-home and is in a chronic campaign to sulkily sabotage every one of her mobile plans. When occasionally Mother is the reserved one, then, sure enough, Father discovers great virtues in hobnobbing with friends, going to the movies and the like.

But it is in the area of withholding sex from Mother that Father shines forth at his meanest or his funniest, depending on one's point of view. When Father complains of impotence problems, the only safe inference to be drawn is that Mother is a woman with an honest interest in sex, whether for its own sake or as the ultimate expression of love. In either case he's got Mother upset and slightly panicked about her basic womanly appeal, and Father sucks up this agitated attention like a powerful dredge. If Mother is a woman who can take sex or leave it with equal ease, then there are never impotence problems, and if there were, nobody would mention them anyway. When, occasionally, Mother drags Father off to one of today's sex clinics for repair of his reluctant organ, the theater of the absurd begins in earnest. The Love Doctors at the clinic, complete with white coats, clipboards and slides, supply Mother and Father with a new vocabulary, of course, and speak softly and sometimes daringly of the many joys of "total union." Ah, those happy endings again. Fortunately for Father's purposes, the dysfunction of his sad sword is sagely diagnosed as a casualty of the stress and pressure of his job, and he has only to work harder on his relaxation techniques to reacquaint himself and Mother with Superjoy, or whatever it will be called this year.

Father is never about to be talked out of his withholding position for very long, or talked into any happy endings for any duration either. Happy endings in any form are acceptable to him only until he begins to feel the loss he knows they eventually represent. The mental-health people, totally addicted to happy endings for their own reasons, are frequently at a loss to explain the apparent failure of marriage and family counseling and will often vindictively diagnose Father as "ineffective," "inadequate," and for really hard cases, though less formally, "a real nothing." But the withholding goes on and not only punishes effectively, but also accomplishes its other major goal of getting Mother's attention: she keeps pursuing him all the more.

One rather sad outcome of all this is the fact that millions of children grow to adulthood actually believing that their parents didn't "get along," as they say. The child of Mother and Father never understands the connection between the two because the child's perspective is vertical, self-centered and literal-minded. The child is also forever incapable of seeing Mother and Father as lovers; the parents are Mom and Dad, almost as if they had been born with those given names. The children see and remember the sulks and the fights, the anger and the retribution, the bitterness and the apparent unhappiness. But Mom and Dad do often stay together, and somewhere in the very core of their nervous systems they both know why – they need each other and they love each other.

What the children are actually witnessing is a strange and savage dance of love and need, which neither party can ever finally concede. As the children grow older, the lovers exploit them ruthlessly, and the kids are never the wiser. The aid and understanding of the children are enlisted by one or the other in this cause or that, and the children go for it with complete and touching sincerity.

Is Father interested in the children? Yes and no. Yes, in the sense that he does have some intense positive feelings for them, which he will show when conditions are right for them to be expressed. No, to the extent that fathering is a secondary process for men, and children are not at the top of their list. Fathering is generally strained through the current state of the sulk at Mother, and he is often content to simply sit and sulk, apparently uninterested in the children altogether. As will be discussed shortly, men on their own have little interest in punishing children, and for the very best of reasons. But when the sulk is not doing the job, Father can become extremely interested in smacking them about, often in direct proportion to their importance to Mother.

Mother, for her part, usually succeeds in making her dogged perseverance in the face of Father's sulk a great virtue in the family, thereby gaining the children's approval. When Mother is a woman whose appetite for the self-serving pain of martyrdom is intense, she can't tolerate happy endings for very long either. Adult children in their thirties and forties are still congratulating Mother for her patience and courage in "putting up with him," and those who have gained the means often show off for her by offering to set Mother up in a nice little place of her own. Mother, of course, declines, explaining with misty-eyed sincerity that she really can't leave him now – it's just too late. The kids proudly leave it as a standing offer. They have bought the whole story.

This appraisal is typical. The children still believe that everything said was true, are still literal-minded about all that went on, and they still believe that Mom and Dad didn't have a thing going. It is simply inconceivable to them that Mother and Father ever rolled around a bed, sweating and moaning together with delight. They believe that certainly Mother and Father would not tell lies to them, or would not give them reasons for things that weren't true. Mother stays because she's just a damned fine person, and Father is angry because he was disappointed and frustrated in his job. And Santa Claus comes every Christmas.

The practical meaning of the long sulk is that it climaxes a relationship between an activist, approval-seeking mother who will assume control of most of her children's activities, and a sullen, sulking father who spends much of his time punishing the mother for her inattentiveness to him and, on a chaotic basis, punishing "her" kids for being a part of it. When Mother and Father then tell the children that they stayed together for their sake, which the kids are always ready to believe to maintain their own feelings of importance, the result is black humor.

There is a professional sidelight which provides an interesting adjunct to this point. In psychology's search for the crucial family background factors which tend to produce schizophrenia, considerable research has uncovered the following pattern: an active and controlling mother paired with a passive and ineffectual father. Sounds provocative? Indeed it does. Perhaps we have unearthed the basic family complex which generates the schizophrenic personality. Just exactly how this pattern produces the personality type is not clear, but perhaps more refined research will ferret out the precise dynamic.

But wait. Other workers seem to have uncovered the same model in parents of the male homosexual. What can this mean? Can it be that these two striking behavioral conditions have unsuspected similarities in background causative factors? Some of the heavier thinkers pursue this provocative hypothesis with diligence and enthusiasm.

Hold it. Good Lord, what's this? Now we find the same timeless pair of lovers lurking in the background shadows of the hysterical neurotic, the alcoholic, the child with rheumatoid arthritis, the passive-aggressive personality and just about every other syndrome ever described. Can it be that we have at last isolated the key psychogenic family factor in the production of *all* emotional problems? Or maybe, just maybe, that's all there is.

3

Do You Take this Man?

According to the dictionary, love is a feeling of warm personal attachment or affection for another person. To possess, by the same dictionary, means to own as one's property. The serenity and peace implied in the first word seems to fit poorly with the bluntness of the second. Right from the very beginning, Father and Mother have plenty of ups and downs trying to get love and possession to fit together in a liveable form. Their struggle has a character all its own long before they are called Mommy and Daddy by little newcomers.

During the inherent contest between them about loving and living, a basic principle of married pairing emerges: One of them loves the other one more; one of them is the seeker, the other one the sought; however narrowly, one of them holds the high cards. Despite fluctuations in this balance over the years, when push comes to shove during a heavy crisis it is generally clear which one is dealing from strength and which one is on the ropes. One of them has lost the capacity to control the other. This kind of analysis sounds shallow and harsh to those who believe that loving should mean that people want to do right by the other one voluntarily, in harmony, without struggle. This may even be close to the way it is when Father and Mother first find each other. Maintaining what they found, however, is the real problem over the long haul, even when the chemistry of the initial match is good, which is generally the case.

Approval-seeking and attention-getting needs provide the basic scorecard for this love struggle in nearly every way, big and small. The various dependencies revealed in each of them are blended into the marital mix and are constantly challenging one of them to forgive the other for needing to be taken care of in a given way. The only marriages which seem to escape the worst effects of the discovery of dependencies are those which take place when she marries a man some ten to twenty years older, the "father image" number, where the needs of the parties make it a little easier to exchange dependencies rather than prosecute for them.

Because approval seeking reveres talking and words while attention getting values action and performance, the lovers are quickly into some difficulties in the management of conflict and struggle. This difference even shows itself in their sexual connection, as we shall see, and aging improves their consciousness and awareness of these stylistic differences only up to a point. Pleasure giving turns out to be just as negotiable a commodity between them as most anything else. Finally, the meaning of their "marriage," itself a separate entity, measures the relative approval value of that state and sometimes makes it a third party living in the home.

In the process Mother learns some interesting things about Father and his ways, some of which please her and some of which vex and irritate her. But Father has also been learning, and he's stumbled onto a couple of profoundly disturbing tendencies in Mother's style which will affect him all of his days. Let's drop in on Father and his woman, before the children come.

Young Marrieds: Frustration and Disappointment

During the first few years of living together the young husband and wife face numerous adjustments, as we professionals like to put it. What are the adjustments we hear about? Precious-sounding things, really, like learning to share responsibilities and feelings, learning to be concerned about another person's happiness and satisfaction, learning to give and take, learning to experience each other sexually, openly and completely, learning to trust each other and accept each other. Summing it up, both have to give up their separateness and merge their personalities and their emotions into "us" rather than "me." The language, as always, is excessive and unrealistic, but it should be clear whose side is portraying the requirements for marriage.

What kind of adjustments are really going on? To begin with, the young husband now has his very own Mommy. He is free at last from competitors, including his own father, and sharing anything is just about at the bottom of his list of priorities. But what is he to do with her? To put it most directly, he plans to lock her up. He is intent on keeping her all to himself and away from the rest of the world. With any luck at all, he will find ways to push out her girlfriends, her work companions and, in really outstanding cases, her family as well. The details of how he goes about it will follow later, but suffice it to note here that the ingenuity and dedication he displays in this cause are awesome.

For the young wife, she is now a married woman, a wife, and, despite all recent attempts to de-romanticize the status, she is enjoying it. She shows off with it in countless places and for innumerable people. She has changed her name and revels in the little practicalities of making that official; often her first small purchase is stationery which puts the world on notice. If she was engaged before the marriage, that is a pure bonus, giving her two shots at the same applause. If she was edging up in her twenties before the marriage, then the applause is intermixed with audible sighs of relief from her family, especially her mother, now that her daughter is "set" and "taken care of." For Mother, the marriage of her daughter is still an anxiety reducer of greater magnitude than tranquilizing chemicals. There is still good reason why the bride's family pays for the wedding.

But now that she's a married woman, a role she's been

prepared for by her mother and her culturally-conditioned expectations, she is intent on creating a home and a wholesome family climate, complete with friends, social activities and, eventually of course, kids. She is also asked sometimes to blend a job or career into the scene, but always keeping the balance among the elements just right. To say that her motives and his are running at cross-purposes is to understate it almost sadistically. And, ominously for the future, no child has yet even arrived in their world.

Whether they have been living together or not before the marriage, the newly-weds have been very busy ever since. During the first few years both are acting out their needs and periodically checking to determine how high their need-fulfillment index is reading. At least as far as enjoyment of the status of marriage is concerned, the young wife comes out slightly ahead in a comparative reading of the charts. How long her slight lead will continue, however, is a very chancy thing.

Some difficult and scary things begin to happen to the young couple. They happen rather gradually for most, very quickly for a few. The big problems are seldom sexual, despite the usual preoccupation with that subject generally. The newly-weds have generally made the basic discovery that two human bodies can be fitted together in the most remarkable ways, and with a sufficient amount of enthusiastic movement, sensations can be produced which surpass anything generated by drugs, amusement parks or Thanksgiving at Grandma's.

Frequently there are money problems, but these are seldom fatal. Besides, in the struggle to determine whose dependencies will win out, money becomes a natural instrument of control, harassment and guilt. The checkbook often flies back and forth between the two of them with dizzying speed, until one of them ends up with it and thereby concedes defeat in that aspect of who will be the child.

There are frequently problems around in-laws and family, but these too tend to be overrated. They have the standard arguments about whose family was better and more wholesome, or, on a bad day, whose the more villainous and disruptive, having caused the worst childhood trauma. But the separate roles for all four of the parents are pretty well mapped out in advance, as will be seen, and for reasons unique to each of them they seldom have any inherent reason to cause problems for the young couple. The fights and difficulties the lovers have about family are usually chronic symptoms rather than causes of their own emotional war.

Their big problem is that they think so differently about the meaning of love and the measurement of it: how one knows when one has enough, or any at all. Attention-getting Father becomes progressively more attached to the obsessive-possessive criterion of loving, while approval-seeking Mother drifts further and further into the more balanced talking, sharing and doing-for standard demanded by that need. They haven't yet reached the point where she feels unloved and he not loved enough, but they are getting there. Eventually the young wife confides to her friends that they are having "communication" problems.

The young husband discovers, for example, that if left to her own devices the woman he married is not going to pay him anywhere near the attention that his mother did. He is going to have to help her along in this regard by dishing up some real unpleasantness. He also finds that she cannot read his mind and, horror of horrors, doesn't even seem to see the need for it and has no interest in trying. She keeps asking him questions about how he feels or what is bothering him, and the very asking has him angry right away because it doesn't lead to reading his mind. If she could read his mind, she would soon know. She would *know*, just as his mother always seemed to. He believes this in his heart of hearts, even if he is feeling very remote from his mother at that time. So much for communication.

The young wife is by this time often stunned to discover that she is living with a child, a baby. He seems to need her to do everything. Long accustomed to the use of a woman, the convenience of a woman who serves, he's a long way from sharing; he's still adjusting to feelings of anger and frustration because his wife doesn't read minds. She finds too that despite his frequent episodes of bluster and bravado, he often lacks confidence in himself when dealing with people, especially authorities, and needs her to do all the talking or complaining. She is often deeply harassed about the household money management too, where he seems to have trouble making up his mind about who should be in charge of the books. She struggles valiantly with all this because there is very little help from her arising from her experience with other men.

If she had a conventionally "good" father who gave her plenty of approval, treated her gently and took good care of her, she is going to find that, by comparison, the man she is now with does very little to boost her own feelings of personal worth. He seems to be all need and only wants *her* to do for him.

If her father was the more common kind of moody and remote type, then she may well be off on a spiritual search for, as women put it, "a man to lean on," "a strong shoulder to cry on," or, sometimes more blatantly, "someone to take care of me." Either way she has plenty of adjusting to do, and the adjustments in question have little to do with the delicate mental-health goals enumerated earlier. They have to do with learning to live with her disappointment and his anger: a collapse of expectations.

Locking Her Up

The natural outcome of the obsessive-possessive loving implicit in attention getting is to isolate the object of love so as to excise all competitors, unless there are special circumstances which alter this rule. Accordingly, the young husband is deeply concerned that an emotional moat be constructed around his beloved, and as quickly as possible. As he gradually realizes that when they are talking about love they are not, at least in part, talking the same language, it dawns on him that she might well resist the moat construction on the grounds that it isn't an expression of love at all, but a hurting kind of interference with her living the life that makes her happiest, in addition to having him, of course.

This conclusion puts the husband in a rather Machiavellian position: he has a goal to accomplish which is of uncertain value to her and which would be impossible to expedite with her open agreement; thus a certain amount of cunning and deception are necessarily involved. That the young husband be entirely conscious of his own motives here is not required at all, and part of the process over the years is for him to learn about himself.

The wife does somewhat the same thing to him, of course, but her version of the lock-up has been substantially accomplished by the marriage act itself.

His first job in constructing the lock-up is to start on her directly. The young husband begins a bit behind in a few key respects. He's not able to show off about being a married man, since undue boasting here would bring suspicious stares from his peers. She is able to draw admiration and respect from being married, and she usually speaks of "my" marriage in a possessive sense, while he talks of "the" marriage, if he mentions it as such at all. He apparently does not see "it" as part of his property.

Before the modern era he could smirk and hint broadly of sexual delights with her, especially if he married a beautiful girl. But these days when sex is being consumerized into tedium, sexual bragging would be old fashioned and unlikely to attract much attention anyway. They have a "sex life" today, just as they have a car and a washing machine. He is simply a husband, and he finds little in the environment to help him make something of it. Whereas she can obtain so much mileage from being married, he can't make a nickel from it, even if he had the need.

He spends a good deal of energy trying to establish himself in her eyes as the resident expert on all things great and small. In days gone by, she might have been able to enjoy the notion that she married a man so smart and so wise and so capable. But these days that is her game too, and together they spend a fair amount of time playing "smartest kid in the class." Catching each other in mistakes sometimes represents a major victory; the middle-class emphasis on grades in school continues into adulthood, and for some couples marks are handed out on a daily basis. His need here is to become the *only* source of input into her head, while hers is to show him how smart she is for approval, or that she is smarter than he is, if she is feeling especially competitive. He will sometimes lie about something to win a point, and thus begins a very bad habit.

His obsessive motive is consistently the same – to occupy her mind with him, preferably favorably, but if not that, then just whatever way he can. His need to lock her up, however, always spreads to other areas, and it's not long into the life of their union before her friends begin to bother him. She pays, he decides, entirely too much attention to them, if not in person, then on the infernal telephone. Then too, in the usual case, she likes to go out on a weekend but often wants a couple or two along to enhance the fun, which creates some interesting options for him. It isn't that he doesn't have friends, but his need for them is of a different nature. He has seldom been graded in the past, as she always has been, according to how many friends he had or how close they were.

His friendships are more openly functional in nature and are often restricted to specific events or activities. His lines of communication with them are far less personal and intense and are usually only tapped for matters of more general interest, as sports and gambling, women and career objectives. Friendships in the first two categories are self-explanatory, and friendships premised on the third invariably involve some unwritten rules. He is under no illusions about his friends at work because they are also his competitors for the same version of the brass ring; if he is an ambitious type, he will not be looking for closeness and fulfillment from his career friendships unless he has missed the point of it all. Recently, a few male groupies of the feminist movement have waspishly denounced these friendships as shallow and unfulfilling, indicating that they never understood the male game in the first place.

In the usual case, he sets out to cast her adrift from her friends by a variety of means. He begins a lifetime of complaining to her about being too exhausted from working to go out in the evening. She will often go for this dodge, even if she works herself. Her own father's life lament has given her excellent preparation for the idea that in some mysterious way the working world is harder on men than women. After all, he has to be the provider and all that. If that isn't sufficient to cancel social life, he will pick a nasty fight with her at seven o'clock on a Saturday evening, thereby ruining the prospective affair, and perhaps even provoking a cancellation. Sometimes he will become sexually active just when she's all prettied up for the evening, and God knows sex can be messy as well as time consuming. She is perplexed at some of his strange and erratic behavior, although still generally willing to accept his explanations.

When she does finally get him out there with some friends for a little fun, there is often no telling just how it will turn out. There are times when he's just fine in public, although he will still occasionally stiff her the minute the door closes behind them and the last goodnight has been said. But there are other times when it is so bad she wishes she had stayed home. She will often be watching him nervously through the evening, even when he's doing well, but when he's in a mood he can be outrageous and "carry on" in public in ways that positively shrivel her approval-seeking roots. He is not above starting an argument right out of the blue, causing a scene, and with enough alcohol he can become downright creative at embarrassing her, causing her to long for the shielded safety of her home. She still tends to see this as personal boorishness in him rather than the isolating tactic it really is. Later, of course, he feels legitimately guilty and sorry – that is until next time.

If the direct assault does not pry her loose from her friends, he will then take a different approach. He will explain to her that they need new friends anyway. These other people would be all right if we were kids, but they just don't make it now. Your friend Jane is really O.K, but her husband Dennis is an insufferable bore with all that stuff about what a big-shot he was in college. And I don't even mind your friend Loretta, she's dumb but she's all right, but her boyfriend Steve is a real jerk shooting off his mouth about his father's money. Before too long he has her doubting some of them herself, because the shortcomings he has targeted were well selected, but she seldom detects the systematic plan behind it. Eventually he may have her down to telephone socials with her girlfriends who sometimes complain, "We don't get together much any more."

As the years pass and she struggles to expand their life with human contact and he fights just as hard to constrict it, if she backs off in her determination to have her friends be a close part of her life, then he may start on her family, depending, of course, on the extent of their significance to her. They have generally been sniping at each other on and off about their families. As a consistent approval seeker, she wants everyone to get along and like each other. He has few preconceptions on this score, but, as always, surveys the environment closely to size up the competitors in the contest to capture her mind.

The most possessive husband generally decides on the straight-ahead route, which he may take even with her mother. He simply decides to have no truck with her crowd at all, and family get-togethers are often marked with a distinct and visible chill, or he will find every possible reason not to attend at all. When she's reduced to making most of the visits to her family by herself, he will then throw every roadblock in her way to make sure she feels as uncomfortable as she can possibly be made to feel. His capacity simply to reject everybody often defeats her because her approval-seeking need has her badly compromised; she is trying hard to please him and at the same time to convince her family that nothing too terrible is wrong. When her family does chance a visit to the married kids, he stiffs them straight out and often will pick that afternoon to shoot a few baskets with his friends. In any case, she finally sees that if she's going to stay close to her family, there's a cost involved. Generally, the telephone gets ever greater use between the hours of nine and five.

Even in the more common case where he decides to accept

some version of strained togetherness with her family, he will somehow let her know his reservations about them. When she asks him what he has against her family, he's always able to come up with something that occasionally even sounds feasible. He studies her indecision closely, of course, and the slightest agreement with his position brings fresh eloquence from him of her family's generally unhealthy, perhaps even destructive, nature. The members of her family rarely understand what is going on and will often search their souls to find any possible wounds they may unthinkingly have dealt him. Even if a conference seems to patch things up, the reconciliation never lasts for long.

Sometimes he even accepts her family with open arms, but in these cases there are special circumstances. If he hasn't had much of a family himself before marriage and his mother was not keen on reading his mind, he often has needs of his own to be someone's child, in addition to hers. Sometimes his in-laws are just super people, which always exerts an influence of its own, regardless of other needs. In yet other cases, he senses that her parents are not all that interested in them anyway and are really more comfortable in keeping their distance. Occasionally, there's money or advantage to be had from her family, and that sometimes makes a big difference to him if he's on the hungry side, but not always.

His dealings with her brothers and sisters generally take on a somewhat different flavor from his stance with her parents. They are not usually the threat to him that her parents are, and at the same time he feels freer to criticize them. He can be ruder and nastier to them more directly and more unresponsive to her pleas for visits with them. His aim, as always, is to increase her overall discomfort in any dealings with them, whether he is involved directly or not. If he's been successful in his job, he really doesn't mind helping out her brother or her sister's husband, once he extracts from her the admission, direct or oblique, that the beneficiary of his welfare is a zero and always has been.

His attempts to lock her up continue fairly chronically through the years, although a total victory is rare. Simply stated, he is jealous of everything or everybody that matters to her, but since jealousy is not "in" these days, it is seldom acknowledged openly. Sometimes, when locking her up makes her too upset and angry at him, he will back off a notch or two until the emergency passes. Sometimes his possessive needs get the better of him entirely, she panics from its gaslight quality, and it will be a short marriage. Regardless of the relative success of the lock-up operation, he consistently demonstrates for her another aspect of the male style which contributes a further erratic element to his behavior, although it is more subtle than the lock-up.

Testing Her Out: The Male Rhythm of Guilt

The young wife has been trying hard to learn about her husband, but it's turning out to be a difficult job. While her approval-seeking engine keeps her straight on course in making herself known to him through all means at her disposal, he often appears as through a foggy window. Trying to grasp the fluctuations of his behavior produced by his attention-getting moodiness is made even harder for her by the fact that superimposed on the moodiness is yet another, even more intricate rhythm, some phases of which hit the depths, while others seem literally to soar into the emotional stratosphere: the rhythm of male guilt.

She feels this rhythm initially when she learns about an interesting difference between them. He can be mean, really mean, in ways she seldom is. During the bad times he can say some monstrous things to her that not only wound her feelings, but leave her thoroughly stunned. He has a nasty mouth, as Grandma might say, and some of the things that come out of it in anger make her wilt and cringe in horror. But then, the next day, or even a few hours later, he will suddenly do his version of "making up," which is now excessive in the opposite direction and take back or deny that he meant any of the vicious things he said to her. When she makes up, she sets things right and in the proper balance again, but when he makes up the affection and benevolence are almost furious in nature, and the velocity of it all takes them well past any point of balance. What's happened? He feels bad after his earlier assault, he feels guilty, and now he wants to make it up to her with the same intensity as the assault-overkill. Many wives report that living with him is either feast or famine, with little in between.

In these days of good-guys, bad-guys, self-help formulae, it is popular to picture guilt as a hideous emotional condition thrust into our psyches by others who manipulate us, past or present, and the guilt must therefore be banished for personal liberation. Not this one. This guilt in the male exists all by itself and is brought on by nobody in particular. The guilt is pure male and develops naturally from the implicit knowledge that he is physically stronger than she and could punch her into pulp at a whim. It gives him the feeling of an advantage over her that, even if never exercised, is always there. When it is used, it generally sets off a chain reaction in him culminating in some very strong guilt which must be expiated. He feels bad because he knows that he's been deliberately and maliciously excessive with someone he truly loves for the express purpose of devastating her and sending her crashing down in tears.

It is not she who makes him feel guilty, it is the inherent unfairness of the situation, or so it seems to him. He knows he has the advantage in that his tolerance for viciousness, even verbal, exceeds hers. He knows he's done something unfair, something almost cowardly. As we shall see for various reasons, he's always ahead of her in knowing about fairness, and her first scent of the same existential guilt usually comes years later, after she has hit her child and feels bad because she was mean and cruel. Because her physical strength relative to others' has not been a basic part of her development, she does not quite see her hitting of the child as cowardly, but she knows somewhere inside her that it is mean.

The self-help books describe guilt as a manipulative tactic, which, for very good reasons, is usually the way she sees it. It's true that when they fight she often states the female version,

"If you really loved me, you wouldn't hurt me like that," which declares her position as the victim at the mercy of the affection of the stronger. And he is somewhat responsive to it, although in most of the fights that isn't the part that makes him feel ashamed of himself. Because children generally and little girls especially live in a dangerous world, to manipulate others by appealing to the same feelings they know in themselves seems the logical thing to do. Everybody is down on manipulation these days, but it certainly has its justification.

Years later as a mother she will sometimes be seen not only as a manipulator, but as a "nag," which is a woman who takes every opportunity to re-state her approval-seeking goals. She is intent on controlling him by the best way she knows. It probably doesn't really work as well as some might think, but it makes her feel better that there is less to be afraid of in the world. When "nagging" graduates to "castrating," as it sometimes does, it simply indicates that she recognizes her man as one who has abandoned any use of the physical differential and can live quite happily with Mommy without having to unleash it.

His need to test her out, to see how tough she is, how much she can take, is what gets the rhythm of male guilt started in the first place. She's interested in his strength too, but for her it seems more a matter of potential protection and relief, or it may be part of a playful sexual image. His interest in her strength, on the other hand, seems more along the lines of a contest, partly with his own strength, but more with some ideal of woman-mother who lives in his fantasies. Each test of how tough she is brings him back eventually to feeling bad about taking unfair advantage of her, and then he charges off in the opposite direction until next time.

The genesis of his need to test her out is complex and obscure. His struggles with his mother certainly make some contribution here, at least in getting the basic swing started. The mid-teen years often bring Sonny into some precarious positions with Mother physically, and the feeling that he would like to punch her out can be intense at times, with predictable shame later on.

Sonny will often "give in" to his mother's demands after un-clenching his fists in sudden panic at the thought. But as volatile as the Mother-Sonny connection usually is, there are additional elements to his need to test her out that seem to be more openly sexual in nature.

Nothing could be more sexually productive and complicated than the fantasies of the fourteen- to fifteen-year-old boy. Sus-pended somewhere between little-kid and grown-up needs, the mid-teens' fantasy life has him on a seesaw about the woman who lives in his mind. Regardless of the varying specifics of names, faces and places, she is sometimes his to use and enjoy on a nonstop, all-out basis. He can always make her have sex by sheer force of personality and persuasion, and she watches him and waits in the wings adoringly with a sure heart. If he hurts her, she is all-forgiving. She lives for him alone, and under her clothes there is only hunger for his hands. But at other times, the roles are reversed and the action becomes a bit on the sado-masochistic side, as the sex scholars have it. It is now she who dominates and rules, sometimes even cruelly, yet somehow still with his best interests at heart; he is now the obedient and docile one, and yet he's strongly secure in her power. It is probably his inability to accommodate in reality either of these early fantasies which gives his need to test out his wife its basic intensity.

And test her out he does. She observes, for example, that he is very childlike in so many ways that she is not. Unless he has had a harrowing childhood of a certain kind, he is very careless about his possessions and clothes, blissfully certain that someone will pick up after him and keep track of things for him. He generally aces her here, despite some serious attempts to train him otherwise, because how the place looks strikes her close to approval-seeking paydirt. He is also capable of some alarming fits of temper when frustrated and will occasionally frighten her by orbiting some objects in retaliation. Chores and errands will be pushed entirely onto her so that to keep any equity going she has to be constantly alert to prevent his bad habits from pushing her over the edge of service into slavery. She's at an additional disadvantage here in that real approval seekers are easily challenged to show just how much work and effort they are capable of.

She learns too that as a married woman she is not allowed to be physically sick; not allowed, that is, if she expects to receive the slightest degree of comfort from him. He seems to take it as a personal affront when she is not well, and often, to her amazement, treats her with an irritable indifference that borders on hostility. He seems to take no pleasure at all in taking care of her and ministering to her temporary needs. Indeed, he often acts as though it were all her fault that she is sick, and one more day of fever will be seen as an overt felony. The really heavy-hitters here are even prone to walking out on her for the evening, leaving her behind coughing, sniffing and utterly crushed. While his irritability is brought on by the attention-getting loss he feels in that her pains are more on her mind than he is, the situation nonetheless represents an excellent opportunity for him to test her out.

The general principle she learns here is that when the woman of the house is not functioning, the inconvenience to all, just by itself, is a source of genuine anger and apparent rejection. His anger at her for getting sick and his challenge to her to toughen up or suffer the insulting consequences leave her approval-seeking needs with only two dreary alternatives: one is to fight all illness and try to swallow her resentment; the other is to drift into a chronic but mild hypochondriasis, which leaves her sick but serviceable and has great prospects for sexual retaliation. When he is sick, on the other hand, it often appears from the tumult that the fate of nations lies in the balance, or at least that smoke is expected from the chimney of the College of Cardinals.

Another product of his testing of her is to add a couple of verbal staples to her vocabulary: givers and takers. She sees herself as the giver, of course, and generally means by this that she is more often the one making the concessions and performing the services in the pursuit of Civilized Living. She is the one who is "giving in," and she often begins to nag, even before she has children, to remind him of his faults and, more importantly, to keep notice of her virtues current. He is seen as the taker who has no grasp of the fairness of service for service, concession for concession. A taker is a person who has the edge in receipt of services rendered. He is not bothered about inequity, and is often called selfish.

She quickly learns not to carry it to the other extreme by spoiling him because he does not handle it very well. If anything, it seems to bring on an arrogance and nastiness of its own. Being a Total Woman works fine for her when she's acting out her own fantasies, but the effects on him are very chancy over any sustained period of time. It seems that he has some strange troubles whenever he's not in the middle between those two fantasy extremes he developed in his teens.

Communication, Trust and All That

Father's been actively learning as well, and much of what he's learned has demonstrated that she literally talks a different language than he does when it gets down to expressing feelings. Their problems on the communication front begin with the same consistent differences in matters of style. As a male, he has a long history of distrust and skepticism about people who are verbally effusive. As a boy, the distrust was originally confined to other boys who talked too much. Some of the skepticism, of course, was tied up with the swapping of lies, and it generally meant that the other boy had crossed the tolerable line on other grounds. As noted earlier, men rarely make an issue of another man being a liar unless the violator has other disagreeable characteristics.

As a grown male, his distrust of verbal overflow spreads from other men to include women as well. It is simply difficult for him to believe that people who talk all that much are not up to something, even if it's just to waste time, as in "talks a lot, says nothing." He is emotionally committed, therefore, to an economy of speech for most occasions, and in any group of men the wariness they show to one of the group dominating the conversation is easily seen. It's an alien style, regardless of the motivation. Professional salesmen are among the wariest of men about excessive talking, and these men are generally the best at it and are reasonably gregarious as well.

Some of his skepticism is generated by the male tendency to watch the environment and events closely; having observed a behavior, he doesn't feel compelled to name it verbally. When she asks, "Do you love me?" he sometimes answers, "Don't you know?" – often not intending attention-getting sarcasm. At other times when she says, "Tell me that you love me. I want to hear it," he wonders what the value of those sounds is to her, even if he is not feeling angry at the time. He doesn't have anything against it as a matter of principle; he just fails to grasp its rewarding significance.

Years later they may have problems of a particular type with a child, perhaps a very young child, only five or six years old. They complain that the child is a chronic liar from whom the truth cannot be squeezed. Clinically, the only immediately correct inference to be drawn about that child is that he lives with people who ask too many questions. There seems to be a kind of law of supply and demand in verbal behavior, which suggests that if any human being meets the demand to talk long enough and frequently enough, he will inevitably begin to lie or else drift into the dreamlike state found in compulsive talkers, entirely unresponsive to anything around them. That much talking simply cannot be done with purity.

Mother's verbal style commonly causes him some difficulty with the expected response. He notices that she sometimes seems to be saying everything that comes into her head, reporting every feeling, acknowledging every bodily twinge, even the smallest, as if her objective were simply to empty out her mind. When she says, "You're very quiet tonight," he is at a legitimate loss for words which might have any possible relevance to anything she has said. Her conversation at these times strikes him as random and excessively detailed, especially about people, somewhat like a small child who pours forth after school a spasm of words, breathless and disorganized, as if the sole objective were to make sure it all comes out. Perhaps no response is really called for.

He has some other problems with her about words, some of them sex words, some not. He notices, for instance, that she commonly talks about "trust" in a relationship as if this were the ultimate nucleus of the love cell. He not only has a very different meaning for that word, but even when he understands what she means by it, he's not at all sure he likes the implication of it. For her, trusting him means relying on his feelings for her, being able to assume that he's not out to do her any harm, counting on some of his feelings as constants in life, which, therefore, she shouldn't have to worry about. Trust means to her that a promise has been made, real or implied, and that breaking that promise will cause her deep hurt. It somehow implies to him that if she could only trust him, his feelings, his promises and his motives then she could keep her energy, enthusiasm and attention free for the rest of married living. The catastrophic implications of this for his attention-getting mind should be obvious, but it's even more than that.

As a man, trusting anybody or anything is a very iffy proposition. To him, trust is a child's concept, when you trust a person not to do you a bad turn behind your back. Also, on a pure physical-safety basis, children learn to trust consistency and to fear unpredictability. The upshot of it to him as a male is that one trusts other people only when the issue at stake is unimportant, but when we are talking about something that really matters, like her, for example, a smart man trusts nobody. He, for instance, doesn't like her alone even with his best friend because he "wouldn't put it past" any guy to make a pass. But she unquestioningly accepts, even delights in, any time he spends with her girlfriend because it implies approval of the friend who, of course, is to be trusted implicitly. That's what a friend means.

It becomes apparent, therefore, that they are often at opposite ends of the pole in this area, and their discussions about their relationship continue to be cloudy and vague. Oddly, he rarely seems inclined to tell her openly that he believes trusting is for idiots, at least when something matters. Ironically, years later as a father, he watches her raising their children where she leaves nothing to chance or trust because they *are* so important to her.

But beyond these problems, which can be frustrating and sometimes angering, he has discovered two large features in her style which have far more important messages for the years ahead. One of these is blatant and flagrant, the other complex and apparently unconscious. In the first place, he's stunned to discover that her concept of intimacy is miles away from his own and, from his point of view at least, in a bad part of town. Intimate to him means private, between the two of them, except of course for his harassment of her in public when the demons reach him. Her understanding of intimate, on the other hand, is definitely not private, but includes sharing with other people, often on a wholesale basis. She ships out facts, information and feelings about the two of them in car-load lots.

He knows for certain that there is at least one other person, and sometimes several, who know every personal detail of his life with her. There are no secrets, he finds, from certain individuals who become notorious to him for that reason alone. He has been made by the outside world. No personal detail is safe from her for rebroadcast purposes, including problems with his boss, his bathroom habits, his brother's prison record, any peculiarities of penis construction and so on, ad infinitum. She has to have at least one person besides him. Her mother, girlfriend and sister lead the list of possible confidantes, or, more commonly, some complex combination of them is employed. But however it's done, he is *known*, and he never quite gets used to it.

He seldom needs such confidantes, for reasons already stated. While he's thoroughly familiar with the lies and often indiscreet boasts men make right from childhood, this phenomenon is something quite different from the intimacy his wife shares with her friend. For him to have such a confidante as a married man would make no sense to him, and to see a man who did would arouse some vile suspicions in him. She tells him that everybody needs somebody to talk to, somebody to pour your heart out to, and he doesn't understand what she means. He doesn't need a third party to discuss the personal details of his life with, not because it wouldn't be masculine, but because he would be completely unable to recognize what the benefits of such an arrangement would be.

What it takes him a few years to grasp here is that the apparently compulsive sharing of details is her rendition of competing, woman to woman, and is one of her primary ways of showing off. She is not about to finish second in the intimacy sweepstakes to anybody, including her own mother. The standards of closeness don't seem to have varied from junior high school, where she and her best friend "told each other everything." The sharing indeed is nearly always an exchange of confidences between the two close contestants, sometimes resembling a daily version of "Can You Top This?" To show off for other women often requires that she demonstrate a level of knowledge about her husband higher than that of other marriages, thereby putting her first in her class. The need for vicarious living is still very strong among women, which further contributes to showing off as a verbal exercise. Because there is little overt performing involved in her version of showing off, it is far removed from his and it takes him some time before he realizes what's going on at all. Even when he finally understands it, it still leaves him mildly dejected.

The second feature of her style that has been revealed to him he finds even more disturbing. What he's learned, little by little, via trial-and-error living, is that, despite her vaunted interest and skill in "communicating," there are some very real limits to what she's willing to communicate about. Her limits here are not really her fault, but she's oversold the communication number rather badly. She started by beseeching him to share his problems with her, but as it turns out, only certain problems are acceptable to talk about. It is usually the other ones which are precisely the troublemakers for him at a later date. If given a choice, she prefers the kind of problem where she can feel instrumental in its solution, either by showing exceptional compassion or intelligent understanding, or both. These problems, the desirable ones, are usually about dealing with other people, helping him work through some job decision, or expediting some practical detail of living.

The problems that she steers clear of, predictably, involve his violent, angry feelings and his sexuality. They often legitimately frighten her, and she will quickly remember a call to be made or that the roast needs checking when he's working himself into either kind of lather. He is not bluffing in these cases as he is when he's off on an attention-getting rampage; his rage now is real and complete. A particularly frustrating encounter or an especially bitter defeat may have him white hot, but he has to control it or she'll run. They haven't been together all that long before he's using ever-more euphemistic and oblique references to his angers until, for some men, they come out completely laundered, without need to be acknowledged.

A few years later, when he feels he'd like to throw the baby through a window, he knows there will be no sharing here, nor any showing off to the girls with that little number, and he goes to work the next morning subdued and thoroughly frightened himself. Jesus, that's maniac country, isn't it? She stays away from him and his feelings when he's into heavy anger because those awful feelings in the pit of her stomach are just too strong. The real limits of her female existence are never closer to her than at those times, or when walking down dark streets late at night. Communication be damned.

Communicating his sexual feelings to her is only slightly easier. Here at least society has set up a busy network of information, speculation and marketing which has made blatant and "unusual" sexual displays if not respectable, at least mildly chic. There aren't even any newsstand vehicles which provide for the vicarious experience of really violent and angry feelings;

some group therapists have invented felt bats and pillows to punch but anybody who benefits from those wasn't really very angry in the first place. If she is a firm believer that sex and love are the same, he's in for some interesting trouble. As will be shown, he's the victim of some fairly extravagant sexual fantasies, which are difficult to express down the straight and narrow, like having her with ten other people watching, or ten other people having her while he watches, or some variation thereof. Thus, if sex has to have a meaning within the context of love, he has a difficult vocabulary problem on his hands that may never see the light of day in open communication. Weird sex is scary too, although a bit less so than anger.

When she's not being frightened by some of his feelings, she's developing some vigorous frustration and boredom of her own. Already vexed by his attention getting and feeling occasionally worn out from the struggle, she often counters with a time-honored cry.

Why Don't You Grow Up and Be A Man?

She often falls back on this cherished standard, even though there isn't much chance that he will know what she means. It is meant as a kind of summary diagnosis of all of his shortcomings, enunciated earlier, together with a hurtful hope that somewhere out there is a stand-up guy with whom a woman could blossom and grow. From the depths of her frequent anguish and frustration, she actually means, why don't you grow up and be like my father, or more likely, what I wish my father had been, or at least like the man I dreamed of when I was fifteen? And what was he like?

"Well, a kind of man who cares, who really cares, who is not above helping out around the house, one who does the masculine chores requiring strength and effort the way they should be done, a strong man, one who doesn't get scared and panicked during difficult times – that's a real man." And there is much more.

"He is a well-balanced man who will get involved with his children and be damned happy that his wife is their mother; a man she can look up to and admire, who treasures her and values her for her own sake; a man she can count on and who's strong for her when she needs him; a man who's willing to sacrifice a bit for her and doesn't always insist on repayment; a man who shows her that he appreciates her for herself as well as for all that she has done for him; a man who is not merely interested in using her, but one who remembers her birthdays and those sentimental occasions that mean so much to a woman.

"And he's a man who comes to her and nuzzles her for no good reason at all. And every embrace from him does not lead directly to probing her crotch and the rest of her equipment. Yes, there can be tenderness and affection, just plain affection – without sex. He's a man who comes up behind her while she's doing a chore and embraces her, saying, 'Hey, Honey, you look tired. How about letting me help?' He's a man who can surprise her, and when asked the reason behind a spontaneous gift, simply replies, 'Because I love you, that's all.'

"He's also a man who brags about her and speaks with obvious pride when women are being compared. And yes, he's a guy who, in the middle of a party, looks across the room at her, and with his eyes alone, says, 'Hey, Babe, you're the best,' and they enjoy their private little intimacy. And when he makes love to her, he does it with affectionate passion, always concerned with her pleasure and satisfaction and eager for the warmth and closeness of afterward. And, finally, he's a man who will set an example for the kids so that they will respect and treasure her just the way he does, and she will never be taken for granted, as so often happens to others."

If Father is confused and ambivalent about what he needs her to be, she seems entirely free of such uncertainty – she wants a real man. The man she seeks, this grown-up fellow her heart yearns for, is a nonstop approval giver, a man who brings peace, not war, a man who gives and shares, not one who demands and takes. He is a man, in short, who has no pressing needs of his own and makes no excessive emotional demands on her, rather like another woman. A far cry, she sometimes sighs forlornly, from the man she got. A far cry, in fact, from all the men who have ever lived outside of dime-store novels and how-to-parent manuals.

And speaking of parenting, that brings us to the baby.

4

Mommy and Daddy: Oedipus Lives here

When Professor Freud's towering genius uncovered the workings of the Oedipal rivalry between Father and Sonny for the possession of Mother, it marked a giant step forward for those interested in understanding the mental life of the child. His keen insight that Sonny was intensely motivated to literally hold on to Mother while excluding Father helped to make intelligible some of the more obscure and provocative behavior of early childhood. This concept of the sexually and emotionally striving child was gradually incorporated into the developing body of knowledge about children and, as the decades passed, the Oedipal theme became a basic idea in the understanding and treatment of the child.

As a purely practical matter, however, the thrust of Freud's creative theory was applied almost exclusively for the benefit of the child. Thus, it was three-year-old Sonny who was to be understood as fearful and often hostile when his needs for the exclusive occupancy of Mother were threatened by the return of great big Daddy. After all, hadn't Professor Freud clearly indicated that Sonny was anxiously concerned about the welfare of his testicles should Father become provoked and irritated by Sonny's attention to soft and cuddly Mother. And it was four-year-old Sonny who was to be humored and forgiven after greeting Father at the door with baleful glance and clear impatience at being interrupted in his private romp with Mommy. Freud's theory made little Sonny's rivalry with and jealousy of Father seem so logical and straightforward, at least on purely possessive grounds, although his suggestions about the child's incestuous hungers for Mother are still regarded as a bit strong for all but the most jaded or liberated.

But Freud's work did precious little for Father. As the society's interest in the child's psyche gradually developed into the mechanical obsession it is today, the emotional life of Sonny's competitor was all but forgotten. "The father" became a static psychological staple defined by the child's perceptions, real or imagined, and as parenting became the busy profession it is hailed as now, the flesh and blood of Father drained out at an ever accelerating rate. To compound the felony, Father's "role," as it is called, became ever more calcified at the hands of the modern masters of mental gibberish into functional slots marked "achievement," "discipline," and the contemporary favorite, "male sex role." Because Freud's perspective on Father was applied entirely from the position of the developing child, it was inevitable that Father would drift finally into the catch-all category of "parent," where he languishes today. Since the approval-seeking standards of exemplary parenthood are "involvement" and "participation," where men perform poorly, the modern critique that Father isn't around for the kids is neatly self-justified.

The final dynamic of the Oedipal struggle produces a powerful general principle of competition and conflict between Father and child (and everybody and everything else as well) for the admiration or attention of Mother: the more closely connected Father is to Mother, the less direct interest he has in the child, and the greater the competitive strife and tension; conversely, the less romantically attached Father is to Mother, the greater his direct interest in the child, and the less the competitive warfare. In the first and more common instance, much of the quality of Father's attention to the child, especially negative attention, is a reflection of his attention-getting, competitive anger at Mother for romantic slights of one type or another. Father's emotional balance, all other things being equal, gives his child-rearing philosophy a highly variable and fluctuating character, because he's often not really responding directly to the child. In the second, less frequent instance, Father tends to be a man who is as much committed to practicality and convenience in living as he is to Mother, and his dealings with the child are less influenced by psychic injuries from her, and more by the desire for direct gratification from the child. As such, of course, he is capable of being at least the menace that Mother can be when she sees the child as a direct extension of herself and her personal destiny. The parent-child interactions of fathers of this second type are, accordingly, more consistent and predictable than those of the first, although that sometimes is not much comfort to the children in question.

When considering fathers of the first and far more plentiful type, Mother and the mental-health experts have great difficulty appreciating this competitive principle, and for the same reasons. Since the goal of both is family harmony and happy endings, it seems illogical and perverse to them that Father should not be similarly inclined. Since Father seldom testifies personally or accurately, Mother often agrees with the experts that there are some fundamental emotional defects in Father as a human being. From the practical point of view of family living, the net effect is still to have a man around with some highly variable and apparently inconsistent views about children.

Father himself has no end of trouble acknowledging the fact that their child has come to occupy Mother's mind to a most disturbing degree. When questioned point-blank about competitive feelings toward the child, Father's "No" is issued with supersonic speed. As a male, he is entirely disoriented by the physical features of the situation to begin with, what with the baby being so small in relation to himself. He feels frustrated and confused by the comparison because it's physically ridiculous. The same lovely "littleness" of the baby which can arouse some deep and primitive twinges of protectiveness in him has him over a barrel when his negative feelings turn up.

Mother, for entirely different reasons, is also unable to be very coherent about Father's competitiveness about the child. The whole idea, in fact, doesn't make all that much sense to her because, after all, the baby is *ours*, isn't it? The baby is the culmination of our love, isn't it? "How can a man be jealous of his own child? That's silly," she says, even when the evidence of such is all around her. She herself has little difficulty with competition of this kind; even when it's little Sis who pushes her and Father apart, Mother smiles, considers it cute and handles the entire incident with ease and grace. The only exception to this is when Mother is seriously narcissistic, in which case she tolerates demotion from nobody, including her child. Finally, Father's consistent denial of the obvious puts the issue to rest for her and allows them both to continue the fight over money, sex, jobs, families and similar basic substitutes.

It is frequently heard in psychological circles that the first-born child is serious-minded, conscientious, responsible, humorless and achieving. As it turns out, he has a lot to be serious about. This is the child who will test the lovers to the fullest. This is the child who touches down squarely in the middle of the love affair still in its purest form; a very special third party is now on board.

The First Child Arrives

What's a "good" reason for having a child? The healthy-living books indicate, predictably, that a loving couple "should" have only one reason, and that is because they are two healthy people who value themselves and others as human beings, who are emotionally "ready" to take on the responsibility, who are committed to being with each other and all that their union brings, and last, but certainly not least, who truly "want" a child. Superhealth strikes again. On the other hand, there is a vast encyclopedia of "bad" reasons for having a child, although as a concession to reality, a little bit of bad is all right, provided that the theme of cosmic mental health described above still dominates. But if your reasons are more bad than good you will almost certainly damage the mental health of the child, and you'll be admitting some pretty shoddy things about the marriage and yourself as a human being to boot.

In real life, however, there is one vital practical flaw in this argument which causes terrible confusion for all concerned, and it is this: neither Mother nor Father has the foggiest idea of what life will be like *when the baby is actually here.* It is truly a novel situation and, as such, the first child is a roll of the dice in nearly every case. This is the reason why the least promising-looking people sometimes make the greatest parents and why some of the golden folks become perfect monsters after the child arrives. Before the fact both sides are living with the abstraction of "the baby" and what it "means" to them. The actuality of the living, physically present baby is often another matter entirely and, for some couples at least, a jarring surprise.

Most modern treastises on having children seem to overflow with a surfeit of altruism and purity of thought which bears favorable comparison with the last utterances of the early Christian martyrs. Such wholesomeness, such thrilling self-denial, such open-armed welcoming of the responsibilities and challenges of the parental destiny. The specialists in "good" reasons have little patience with real life, and inherent in all their words is an elaborate system of clever criticism and approval-seeking projection disguised as expert opinion. The premise is that Mother will be called upon to give her reasons for wanting the child to others; in approval-seeking terms, young Mother has to buy the whole package because owning up to anything resembling a "bad" reason might bring her some attention from her peers, but certainly no approval. Sometimes, in serious post-partum depression, a deeply frightened girl is brought face to face with the baby and finds her "good reasons" disintegrating under the weight of a few "bad" ones she's tried so hard to suppress.

What about those bad reasons anyway? Why is it that they often turn out to be no different in practice than the good ones?

What actually happens is that the first child is one of the most profound learning experiences in the human lifespan – not just learning about the baby, but learning about oneself. Consider some of the bad reasons for having a child: to save a shaky marriage, to have one's own personal toy, to rescue life from boredom, to create another human being to achieve what one did not, and all similar selfish reasons head the list. But all of this refers to feelings before the birth, and the predictability of "good" parents from the stated reasons for having the child is nowhere near as accurate as we are led to believe. Part of the reason for this lies in the definition of "good parenting," but even more of it is attributable to an underestimation of what will be learned with the first child itself.

These simple-minded predictive fallacies are everywhere in the parent-child industry. Child abusers, we are told today, are simply people who themselves were physically brutalized as children and who now act out the same script with their own. Would that it were all so simple, but, alas, there are few rules that hold up here. Some of the most flagrant child-punchers never felt a hand during their own upbringing, while many who were pummeled unmercifully as children have absolutely phobic prohibitions against ever hitting their own. It's the same intellectual sleight-of-hand which tells us that the young men who splatter old people all over the sidewalk do that only because they are poor and drug-addicted. Great insight, wrong problem, but it sounds so complete.

Unlike the experts, Father has begun to discover some things about himself and how he is likely to behave later with Mother and child even before conception. Despite all the current talk of planning the baby, Father often toys with the peculiar thrill of "knocking her up" on a somewhat more spontaneous basis. He often gets downright careless about the birth-control plan. Yes, he thinks, doing something "to her" rather than "with her" has some powerful appeal to him, and he often finds the birth-control routine vexing to him for dark and vague reasons. Now, "knocking her up" would most assuredly fall high on the main list of bad reasons, but when Father has Mother naked on the mat, the health book is far removed from his mind. And unless young Father is preoccupied with money and security, he's gradually edging most of the birth-control responsibility onto Mother anyway, hoping thereby to maximize his romantic pleasure, while still saving the blame for her if anything goes wrong. Sometimes the pills, jellies, foams, condoms, diaphragms, devices and contraptions fly back and forth between the two of them in their unique game of bedroom tennis. Planned parenthood indeed.

The same notion of doing something *to* her is carried over right into the delivery room. Some fathers, rather passionately linked to their women, will take the course so that they can be present during labor and the actual birth. Part of this motivation is that Father is near suffocation with terror about anything happening to her, but another part of it seems a bit more on the purely interpersonal side. The intellectual, natural-living crowd find this inspiring and indicative of a man who's not afraid to challenge boldly the male stereotypes, thereby showing himself to be a caring, sharing guy. The thought that Father might be enjoying Mother's pain while she, in her turn, shows off the ultimate human capability is quickly dismissed as insensitive and perverse.

Young Father also discovers that the baby has provoked emotions in him that he does not recognize as familiar from his past repertoire. He often feels a mixture of affection, jealousy, fear, protectiveness, curiosity and other indefinable elements quite unlike anything he's experienced in the past. Who could ever have guessed, he reflects, that these feelings could have come to him. It's certainly different, all right, and his first few months of fatherhood are often spent just thinking about what he's feeling. But while he's trying to figure out what these feelings mean, there is still time for him to be keeping a close eye on Mother and where her attention is at any given time.

So, all of the literature and discussions about "good" reasons for having a child turn out to be scant preparation for the real

thing. It appears that the good-reasons-for-having-a-child market advice is pretty much the same thing as just about every
other issue in the parent-child lecture series: it tells Mother what
the "right" answers are, the approval winners, in group discussion. It's still usually a sexual thing to Father, but then again
his reasons for wanting the child may not have been a basic part
of the discussion anyway. When pressed, Father indicates his
agreement with the good reasons by mumbling, "Well, we're
ready to start our family," and that generally satisfies the
listeners.

Father learns that his first trouble with Mother about the
baby arises from an entirely unanticipated source, which proves
most difficult to deal with: the baby makes Mother very anxious
and nervous. She's an amateur at this, of course, and Spock's
book helps somewhat by reminding her to calm down. She's still
tense, very tense, and is often staggering from fatigue because
she can't sleep with one ear and a half listening for sounds from
the baby. That she worries about the baby reassures Father,
because that's a sign of a good mother to him. At the same time,
however, his direct attention index from her is sliding to dangerously low levels. His "immaturity" is starting to show, and
her anxiety about the child is beginning to reach him in some
novel circumstances.

Sex, for instance, is one of the first casualties. On more than
a few occasions, just as Father is getting down to some serious
sexual delicacy, the baby gurgles, Mother stiffens, leaps up and
hastens to the crib. Father, erection akimbo, is left seething at her
abandonment and speculates darkly at the fact that the baby is
occupying her mind more than he is; he is losing the competitive
struggle to own Mother's mind. In true attention-getting style,
Father feels the obsessive loss even if Mother happens to hurry
back to bed to finish the job. The competitive rank order is
getting established along a very slippery track.

The baby's sleeping and crying habits soon come to have great
significance because of the anxiety they provoke in Mother. It is
still usually Mother's job to get up with the child during the

night for maintenance chores, but this makes Mother's sleeping schedule more erratic and out of sync with Father's needs. Sure enough, he calls her during the day, and she's asleep. In some cases Mother only sleeps when the baby sleeps. Father is getting more irritable by the day because Mother is becoming progressively less available to him, and the competition is taking a dramatic turn for the worse. But these chores have to be done, Mother snaps, and Father is not able to talk that one away. Mother, for her part, would like some good old-fashioned approval and appreciation for her fatigue rather than the irritability and rejection which seem to be developing.

The baby's crying is another matter. Should the infant be picked up and cuddled? or should the crying be endured after checking obvious sources of distress? As a stress stimulus, the sound of a vigorously crying baby is easily the equal of any; over any extended period of time it brings the human nervous system into contact with its outer limits. Experts on this type of situation abound, of course. If you always pick him up when he cries, it will spoil him forever; if you don't, he'll be grumpy and a little paranoid all of his days – take your choice. Mother generally decides to pick him up and often meets an animated lecture from Father about spoiling: toughen him up, nothing is handed to you in this world. If she decides against picking him up, then Father is at her for being cold, unfeeling and probably lazy. Young Mother usually takes what Father says as his "position" on the matter, rather than seeing that Father's "position" is simply the opposite of hers and has little to do directly with the child. As in so many of their encounters over the years, Mother has a policy, Father has a reaction.

Father's counter-attack is directed at Mother, regardless of her mothering policies, but because she takes what he says too literally she often reaches some depressing conclusions about Father. His erratic philosophies about children and life and his moodiness, which is generally ascribed to his work, provoke her to believe that Father is simply not interested in the infant. Generally, Father is aware that he is more interested in her than he is in the child, but Mother is singularly bothered and depressed by his relative lack of interest in their first creation. Her depression is deepened if one of her girlfriends has a man who seems to enjoy sharing the care of their baby; she is somewhat comforted later when her own mother points out that men in general are more like Father. Through it all, Mother is in need of some approval as a mother and comforting affection as a woman. But even getting affection is a sometimes thing, and sex itself seems to have gotten so damned complicated.

Sex Takes A Fall

Mother is so right; sex between her and Father has certainly become complicated since the baby arrived, and it generally stays that way. The reasons for the complexity are many, varied and often extremely subtle. What is a "good" sexual relationship in a marriage anyway? The country's experts have answered in droves, and the overall answer, as expected, incorporates every superlative imaginable. The happy-ending theme is everywhere, of course, beginning with mutual desires, proceeding to equal desire and finishing with the simultaneous orgasm. There are some couples who can do it just that way pretty regularly, but for most, the sexual priorities are seldom mutual, and the happy ending remains elusive, often actively rejected by one of them or both.

There isn't much help for Father and Mother from the recent flurry of sexual surveys either. They are all propaganda, and the major theme seems to be about what Father is really like as a man. Some say he's really just like Mother sexually, with the strong belief that love and sex are twins, that marriage is the preferred state, and that his major concern is really pleasing Mother to the fullest in the simultaneous orgasm.

The other side maintains, however, that their surveys clearly show that Father is really just a penis surrounded by functional protoplasm, and their results substantiate the vile view that

Father would mount a snake were it properly defanged and the lighting right. The first set of researchers is obviously trying hard to make official the unisex version of the famous sexual revolution, and the second group seems intent on giving some social and psychological status to their ambivalence about the importance of Father's organ.

The real-life truth lies elsewhere, as usual, and still revolves around the basic sexual differences between Mother and Father. Understandably, they do quite well where they are alike; it is their differences which are at the root of their fluctuating sexual fortunes. Mother reports, for example, that a sexual overture to her after a nasty fight often provokes another fight just as bad; her head is turned off, and it's slightly disgusting to her that he can so easily get into that stuff after what's been said. Sexual revolution or no, Mother is still very much concerned with the relationship aspect of sex, and Father's urges sometimes strike her as random, animalistic and indiscriminate. It still has to "mean" something to her; there has to be love and affection, and patience and time, and perhaps even mutual agreement as to the meaning. Father is also interested in the relationship part, but often sees her view as a demand for gratuitous surrender of some piece of his masculinity – namely, his ability to "make" her, to talk her into it. He was often able to do that before the baby came but he's seldom able to now. Mother's reluctance now seems more genuine than it used to be, for some reason.

The child itself comes to be a major sexual deterrent for many couples. When the baby comes home from the hospital, where he sleeps becomes important. If the crib is in their room, sex takes on a novel touch; there's someone in this room with us. One of them discovers a touch of squeamishness at this unexpected exhibitionistic problem, and it's more often Mother. Father usually doesn't seem to mind, and in some cases is even aroused a bit by the concept that there's someone there, perhaps watching. Perhaps they wonder if it will mess up the baby's mind if he awakens to the sound of the thrashing.

When the child is older and more mobile he becomes a

potentially more dangerous guest. Toddlers are famous for wandering around at the strangest times and, of course, the first place they make for is Mother's bedroom. These are the times of door locks and devices, and sex is now undertaken with a good deal more deliberateness and cautious tension. In earlier times, some analysts believed that witnessing Mother and Father in the sex act represented a trauma of violence to the child. If that were so, one doubts that television would ever have got a start. Some experts believe that Father's later problems with voyeurism had their beginnings while he was loitering outside his mother's bedroom door, straining at the keyhole to catch the sounds. What's going on in there? In any event, the kids are not sexual stimulants for Father and Mother, to say the least, and they force some degree of sexual compromise as to time and place under any conditions. The lovers are no longer free.

They also have differences and troubles about the words to be used, as has the entire society for eons. These days Mother's favorite is "making love," and that will generally do for most purposes, but Father sometimes gets bogged down in semantic confusion generated by that term. For simple, straight-ahead urgency, Father thinks of "screwing," while "making love" implies something more exotic, with heavy overtones of enthusiastic and conscientious oral sex. Eating and sucking is more to the point, he feels, but in close-quarters contact, these words can jar Mother and sometimes distract her entirely from the immediate enterprise. The sexual revolution was supposed to have done away with that kind of squeamishness and made plain words a common part of everybody's vocabulary. In social talking that may be true, but in close intimacy country, that is still definitely not the official language. And then too, aging and responsibilities still make people conservative, as they always have, and it isn't very long before Mother is getting impatient with too much verbal flexibility of that type.

A strong case can be made for the idea that sex education in elementary schools really got started because of vocabulary problems, when Mother simply got fed up with her children's (especially Sonny's) chronic use of the word "cock." Mother banded together in the local school districts with those who wanted the kids to learn that sex is beautiful and not dirty, filthy and disgusting, to produce an odd vocabulary course for sixth graders, taught by some very nervous teachers. Sounding for all the world like a lesson in early Roman architecture, the little ones learned about vaginal walls and penile erections and even, occasionally, the various positions of intercourse. At a slightly later age, especially in the more "advanced" school systems, cunnilingus and fellatio were added for an exotic flavor, although the verb forms remained difficult for even the brightest students. The kids learned it, smirking all the while, since they enjoy talking about it any way it's dished up. That there have been few recorded instances of lovers actually saying these exact words to each other mattered not at all; it was the habits of social conversation that were at issue.

In high school the emphasis shifts slightly to cover the serious problem of unwanted, unknown and uncalled-for pregnancies. Cycles and charts abound, with blackboard-length diagrams and audio-visuals of stages and openings, cavities and canals. The psychological theme is developed that sex is a matter of the utmost seriousness and should only be undertaken after extensive soul searching and a mature decision and commitment to one's partner. Sonny and his cronies, meanwhile, sit nervously in the class and worry about how to get the masturbating down to twice a day. Sex isn't dirty anymore, but it sure has gotten verbose.

Finally, at college-level and adult, human-sexuality courses, the talks turns to more spiritual matters like how much of ourselves do we give when we give our bodies, why sex has to mean something between the partners, the basic nature of a sexual relationship, or infatuation as compared with a real love relationship. The leaders of the course are usually hip and liberated middle-class, social-science types who ache to relieve themselves of early repression and to show off by bringing the class face to face with sexual reality. Let's throw off the facade of conventionality, they urge, often after catching the latest sex training film, invariably "sensuous," featuring someone slowly gyrating the small of the back. Let's be real people, let's say it like it really is, let's use street language to talk about sex. Let's all grow up and be like the real people, the street people. Let's all say *cock* and *cunt* right out loud. Gee, isn't this fun, right back where Sonny started from.

These days, what "pleases" Mother or Father is seen as the very heart of the matter and, of course, has turned into a complicated and often difficult negotiation, with frequent exasperation and frustration on both sides. Mother is generally committed to the idea that it takes a woman longer to heat up, so that the lovemaking is premised on allowing sufficient time for Mother to turn to broil. Exactly what happens, how it's done and how long it takes during this interval becomes crucial. The sex books call this period foreplay, the prefix implying its systematic nature, the suffix still holding out hope for the idea that it might yet be fun. What is clinically called oral sex becomes the focus of concern at this point, and Mother and Father seldom agree about the esthetics here. Their appetite for each other's juices is at issue, and whichever of them is the more finicky and fastidious generally has the other bothered by the lack of enthusiasm so clearly shown. Accordingly, one of them always seems dissatisfied at the point where foreplay becomes foul play, with there being too much of it or too little, as the case may be. The same oral issue is often of central significance during Mother's menstrual periods and the last couple of months of pregnancy. How to get Father off (and Mother too sometimes) becomes vital, and the resolution of it becomes part of the couple's sexual pattern.

Within the animated discourse of satisfaction and pleasing in today's orgasmic age, the invitation to all manner of ploy and counterploy, withholding and counter-withholding becomes ever more overt. Thus, when the marriage mechanics solemnly advise the young never to use sex as a weapon in marriage, the projection of unreal people in an unreal world sounds not merely sanctimonious in a mental-health sense, but they crystallize the happy-ending theme into immortality. Sex, they say, is not a game, not really fun at all, but a serious business of pleasing and satisfying. Positions of intercourse should be changed and tried for greater closeness and satisfaction, and whatever little twists on the familiar which might increase pleasure should be freely exchanged. By golly, it's almost like working. But changing intercourse positions probably won't help much. Father is often lost in this format because it misses a few essentials of his entire sexual orientation, which is almost always inherently kinkier than hers.

Mother has discovered that while Father is attracted, sure enough, to the front of her, as the supposed breast culture suggests he should be, his interest in the back of her is a good deal more than casual. The discovery of Father's love affair with Mother's buttocks occasionally unnerves her entirely. Good Lord, what the hell is this? Since approval seeking is basically a face-to-face, up-front proposition, showing one's backside does not really fit into that system. To make matters more delicate, Mother may have read somewhere that if Father shows an excessive interest in her rear end, it may mean he's a closet homosexual, because the rear view tends to homogenize the sexes. The fact is that unless Father has been crushed as a boy by too much virtue of a certain type, he will happily enter Mother through any of her openings without the complex esthetic or practical decisions Mother has to make. As things now stand in the sex books, showing undue affection to Mother's behind stands somewhere between unusual pleasure and mild depravity.

While these specific factors can cause enough trouble on their own, the biggest sexual stumbling block between the two has little to do directly with specifics; it has to do with Father's disturbing sexual fantasies, which have been with him from his teens. The mental life of the fifteen-year-old boy shows this age to be as wild and volatile, creative and expansive, intense and complicated as any age before or after. While the sex trainers feel they have done their noble best after they have assured

Sonny that masturbation is really O.K. for a fellow, provided he doesn't spend all day in his bedroom or bathroom, they never get to where the jackpot is, the accompanying fantasies.

And what fantasies they are, both in range and content. Incessant dominance-of-women themes vary with submission-to-women ones, and the girls in the fantasies are in whatever mood fits the need. Voyeuristic fantasies also appear for un-fathomable reasons to Sonny, where he's watching it done rather than doing it: the harbinger of Father's most persistent and disturbing fantasy twenty years later. Season young Sonny's mental-sexual tumult with an occasional homosexual theme and the fantasy cauldron is at full bubble, and it will remain so for a long time to come. Also at this time, magazines with pictures of females in the buff begin to exert their voyeuristic effect and can be found everywhere around his room, as they will years later after he's a father.

The teenage fantasies of Sis, masturbating or not, are still very much of the love-relationship sort, where the fantasy has a plot and some type of happy ending. Oh yes, there's the occasional fantasy of being raped by a rock star or sudden sex on a midnight bus with a stranger playing a guitar, but the "sweet surrender" theme is still the bread-and-butter drama for Sis, and its meaning stays pretty close to those limits. While Sis may be masturbating often enough, it doesn't obsess her as it does her brother, and always it seems that pleasure can only be achieved fully with the "right" fantasy.

Masturbating as a grown woman has little inherent appeal to Mother, despite recent efforts by some belligerent urban types to provide regular classes for women on how better to get off alone. Mother sees masturbation as an occasional necessary evil, but to develop skill and expertise at it would be much too threatening to her. Whether coming or not, it would only remind her that she's doing it by herself, and the loneliness of it would collide head-on with her approval-seeking disgust and anxiety at doing anything alone. No, the masturbation classes won't sell, because they would be telling Mother something she doesn't want to hear and will certainly not pay to take lessons in. Coming be damned.

For Father, however, it is quite another story. As the years pass and he and Mother work their way into their particular sexual pattern, the teenaged fantasies return with renewed strength, and Mother's consistent real-life rival is now not another woman at all, but Father's fist. One-half of center stage in Father's show is occupied by those shadowy girls of his youth, now recostumed to fit the period, or Miss Jones at work, or Jack's wife Barbara, all with saucy mouth and eager eyes. Father can perform sexually with Mother in the bed, while the split-screen shots in his mind have him simultaneously down the block inducing another surrender among thousands. Will Father ever admit that he's back to masturbation? Almost never! Likewise with impotence. When the subject comes up, he'll just claim that overwork and pressure have driven his desire down. More creative and hostile men will claim impotence from mysterious spiritual demons, probably unleashed by Mother. The other star of Father's fantasies is Mother herself.

While the male voyeuristic theme catches Father the hardest if Mother is out playing around, it does carry a certain fascination for him. Sometimes, even when Father is quite young, he will banter with Mother about her attentions to other men, real or imagined, or even jokingly suggest during times of tension that an affair would do her some good. Mother usually smarts from these suggestions, apparently offered in a malevolent good humor, "kidding," as Father later puts it, but sometimes she notices that Father is inexplicably nervous when talking about this seemingly odd subject. It is somewhat the same nervousness Father's "other woman," if he has one, notices when he launches into a detailed description of Mother's sex life elsewhere, if she has one. Talking about Mother and sex in combination often appears to be as exhilarating for Father as doing it.

Mother herself is seldom voyeuristic beyond reasonable limits, so that much of this doesn't make any sense to her at all, and, at the relevant times, she's inclined to diagnose Father as being "a little crazy." She does note that Father often complains to her that he wishes she were more sexually aggressive and that she would take the initiative in their couplings, but she generally regards this as the expression of a practical need rather than any fantasy hype. Father's fantasies, however, demand that Mother be seen as a sexual woman with relatively chronic interests in sex, so that he won't feel that he's the only one. Thus, aggressive and initiative are his favorite words when his fantasies are blending into reality a bit. If Mother does happen to be the initiatory type, he will often become a withholder in order, perhaps, to edge his fantasy that she will be compelled to fulfill her needs elsewhere a bit closer to reality. Sometimes when making love Father and Mother exchange fantasies, and Mother plays the game along with him about those other men present in the game and what they are there for, although Mother is still left wondering if he's for real about this.

Mother is usually the one who discovers, on a straight, practical basis, that if Father wants her three times a week and she wants him twice, sex twice a week may lack some esthetic appeal, but it works better. Father is still in the position of pursuing her, which turns out to be sexually essential, and the exact ratio of pleasing and satisfying is often an up-and-down thing anyway. When the shoe is on the other foot, and she wants him more than he wants her, there's trouble ahead for several reasons, not the least of which is that Mother gains no great thrill of self-esteem by being the pursuer. It's fine as an occasional kick, but as a steady diet the inverse sexual-desire ratio simply doesn't work well. In addition, when Mother is the sexual seeker, it creates temptations and opportunities for Father to fool around with her mind either on a punishment basis or else as part of his fantasies about her sexual needs taking her elsewhere.

No, Mother decides, better not to spoil him; Father does not handle emotional or sexual success with her all that well. She's generally right about that, even though that conclusion tends to violate the hysterical goals of total union. There does seem to be a necessary and vital tension in a marriage, wherein one of them is somewhat dissatisfied and seeking and the other one can be described, temporarily at least, as having the upper hand. When one of them is spoiled, for whatever reason, there are troubles, although Father's sins tend to go in different directions than Mother's under these circumstances.

If the tension gets too far out of hand and their respective needs don't mesh often enough, then the thing collapses of its own weight. When the tension level is somewhere between the two extremes, they stay oriented to each other, however obliquely; a good part of the behavior of each is directed at the other, and they have some facility to come together, especially after times of real stress between them.

Building Life Around The Child

After the first child arrives, and regardless of how many may follow, the process of organizing their lives around children starts in earnest, and the developments during these years pose serious threats to Father's attention-getting needs. Mother's time to shine is here for sure, and her needs to show off in her own way are soon in full flower. It is certainly not without its problems for her, but it's her stage and she's got it pretty much alone. The showing off takes many forms, to Father's eye, from the practical and obvious to some high-level assaults on him.

When the first child, or any child, is new, the showing off is overt, and even Father himself can have some excellent moments just watching her. Visitors invariably hope to tiptoe into the child's sleeping place to have a look or, if the infant is awake, to have a hand at holding and jostling him, perhaps even eliciting a smile. If the child is especially attractive, the showing off becomes all the more exaggerated, but even a plain baby will do the job. She is now a Mother and in a sense achieves a major life goal at a tender age; for Father it would be like becoming Chairman of the Board at twenty-five. While the organized man haters and woman haters in the society snarl and rip at her role, the rank and file still recognize the ace of spades when they see it.

One of the most fundamental changes which occurs in their family is a reassessment of expertise. It's actually been going on before but reaches high gear after the baby arrives. Mother's obstetrician and pediatrician have become important figures in her life as the experts on her and the baby's bodies and all manner of things, including Father, and their conversation often takes on a strangely conspiratorial quality. At dinner Father is confronted with the doctor's expert opinion that two martinis before eating definitely indicates an alcohol problem, just as she's been saying all along. Father often feels that gratuitous opinions such as this must be resisted with vigor, because he's very anxious that the doctor's expertise be restricted to his area of training, namely Mother's body or the baby's body, rather than the world at large, especially his part of it. But in nearly all cases the physicians are Mother's allies in contested family matters with Father.

While Mother's doctors are a relatively small part of the couple's life, their input consistently signals a gradual exclusion of Father as an *expert* on anything. Mother is looking to him for knowledge and expertise less and less. Other forces going in the same direction join this one, and Father increasingly contends with some serious image problems. Initially, the main concern Father has is that the doctors take good care of Mother and the child, and he doesn't notice that slowly the doctor's area of expertise is growing without benefit of further schooling. This has nothing to do with Mother's occasional flirtations or fantasies if her pediatrician is a man who shows off his authoritative charm for her, nor is it that Father feels the doctors are replacing him in any objective sense. They are simply part of a package whose most vital point is Mother's emergence as the resident expert on everything to do with the child, including fathering.

How Mother becomes the acknowledged authority on good and bad fathering is a complex matter which Father seldom challenges. From his point of view, no matter what anybody says, the child came out of her body, not his, and that's that; no elaborate theories or explanations need to be supplied. Accordingly, no matter how well he debates her about his role, he still comes off with an amorphous feeling of angry guilt. Yes, Mother knows what's best for the kids, not only from her but from Father as well. Whether Father has done right by the kids, is a matter of instant intelligence to Mother, with little chance of effective rebuttal. This unvarying script is often acted out in the divorce court, where Father often stands accused by Mother and her fearless attorneys, demanding to see a photostat of a check for summer camp and usually also by the judge, whose aggressive wholesomeness in the children's behalf wanders between the comical and the pathetic.

Interestingly, Father almost never raps Mother publicly for being a bad mother, even in cases involving overt neglect and abandonment. Of course he often tries to harass her privately for some attention-getting advantage, but in front of others it's almost unheard of. Even when the child is getting some heavy neglect from Mother, Father simply says, "She's just not taking care of the kids," and worries about what to do, since he seldom has any easy solutions. It's probably a good thing he doesn't, because even children abused at Mother's hands startle the social workers by their adamant refusal to reject her as "unfit." When Father does attack Mother on grounds of unfitness, it is almost always when she has got a new man in bed with her, and Father rather foolishly alleges that this sort of shameless pleasure will permanently upset the kids.

Once Mother appoints herself to the job of on-premises expert on fathering, and Father unconsciously concedes the promotion, she is then able to show off to him and the world at large in a greatly increased number of ways. When Father denies her superior expertise, he sporadically tries to compete with Mother on her terms, and the results for the child are predictably bizarre, with two energetic impresarios of "love" now hustling the audience from the same stage. That a contest should develop is as good a comment on the times as any.

In fact, Mother has no more idea of what a "good" father is than Father does, nor do the experts, for that matter. They are both limited by their personal experience with their own fathers, and on balance Mother may come out slightly better here simply because she was better at staying out of trouble with him. Mother has never been a male, and so would have no way of knowing what the unique factors of maleness mean with children, just as Father wouldn't know the reverse. As we can see, all that can ever be made sensible are certain minimums of behavior from either of them, which goes down hard in a society hungering for parental superlatives and other showing-off equipment.

The practical result for Father is that he's often angry at Mother on the entire fathering score, but now his choice of retaliatory measures becomes obscure and confused: attack her or "her" child? Which? Or both? Since Mother has appropriated the welfare of the child as her own, the options for Father are at once expanded, but agonizing in a novel way. His oblique resolution about the child, often on the hostile side at least, takes the form of "teasing" and "kidding" the child until the tears come, sometimes including Mother's as well. Stepfathers, because they face even greater competitive stress, become masters at this nasty habit. They can also twist their temper neatly in other directions by offering to adopt Mother's child, complete with name change, which effectively puts Mother over that proverbial barrel and disguises all kinds of little angers. The child, as always, is assumed to be a perfect zero in the equation.

Father's offensive against Mother, however, continues along pretty regular attention-getting lines. Going out for an evening now provides a more interesting setting for Father to enjoy her or punish her, as the case may be. If he's hungering for some time alone with Mother, then he will move heaven and earth to get the time out from the baby expedited, complete with acceptable baby sitter. The baby sitter indeed becomes a key part of the whole transaction, and to some degree her competence is a major issue. If they go out but Mother finds her mind wandering back to the child's welfare at the hands of the hired help, requiring some phone calls to control her anxiety, then Father is soon in a sulk – ostensibly because the food is lousy. If Mother has developed into a real stay-at-home, then Father suddenly discovers the virtues of stepping out and hounds her about their mutual need for a break to relax them from all the pressure. If Mother retains her interest in hobnobbing with her friends, however, then Father will line up with the child and find it unconscionable that she is so willing to trust their precious child to the care of mercenaries.

The same variety of script is acted out when they have to decide on a vacation. When they go by themselves, leaving the child behind in the care of someone else, Mother's anxiety will be the key to the trip. If she's worried about the child, the telephone gets a big play, and Father finds numerous faults with the hotel, the climate and the people. If the child is not causing Mother's mind to wander, as when he is being cared for by her mother, Father has a good time. At these times Mother easily notices what a good mood he's in and attributes it to the vacation and relief from career pressure. On the other hand, if they decide to take the child along, Father's mood is a good deal more variable. Such trips often get cancelled at the last minute because something of top urgency has arisen at the office, and Father simply can't ignore it. I'm terribly sorry, he says, but maybe another time soon. Father, as usual, has been watching Mother's desire to be with him; sometimes it looks good, and other times it falls short. When her desire falls short cancellations, illnesses or urgent last-second commitments will generally materialize out of the blue, with a speed that would make Merlin nod with approval.

Sundays at any given time of the year also provide close views of the same struggle. The purpose of the Sunday drive is to wander around at a leisurely pace, perhaps dropping in on a friend or doing a little casual shopping. The result is usually quite different, with Father snarling and cursing at other fathers, when he speaks at all, occasionally flailing at the kids in the back seat, while Mother sits alongside trying hard to conceal and control her own apprehensions, lest the children aggravate him into foaming at the mouth. Her attention index to him and the children before and during the drive is generally the most important regulator of his mood, and if her relative priorities are poorly presented that day, Father can be a real menace out on the road. Only the snarl of traffic which prevents high speed keeps the wreckage down, literally and otherwise.

The Oedipal struggle with his own children gives Father his most anguished moments for most of his life, and his resolution of the situation varies sometimes from day to day. Father as a man loves his child, but the stress of losing Mother's attention is truly angering to him and, worse luck, the loss is to another of his own beloveds. His other major competitor for Mother is generally her mother, but here the problems presented and the resolutions available are somewhat different from when he's competing with Sonny and Sis.

The Return of Mother's Mother: The Grandparent Effect

When adopted daughters grow up, marry and become pregnant for the first time, they often report a vivid and intense desire to search for and find their natural mothers. The urge seems unrelated to her previous feelings about searching or whether her relationship with her adoptive mother was close or estranged. The feeling she has is that she needs her mother, and the production going on inside her own body often brings these longings to top-priority status. From all observations, adopted or not, she is right, because Mother's mother thereby becomes a much more significant element in Father's life when the first child is born, regardless of where she was earlier.

His wife's need for her mother actually seems fairly reasonable to all but the most possessive fathers, and in many cases, Mother's mother has been a functionally integral, if physically peripheral, part of their family for some time. The stirrings of motherhood seem mysteriously sufficient to have Mother in greater need of the person she trusts and relies on so much for emotional support. The first child brings anxieties and concerns that seem to be most easily soothed by a same-sex person of more mature years. Because Father is a bit scared himself, he's not that averse to seeing Mother buddy up a bit closer to his mother-in-law. Her mother is almost always a unique and special case from among the four parental possibilities in the situation.

Her father, however, is a different cup of apple juice. Generally her father is little trouble because he's really not that interested. He's glad his daughter is well married; his son-in-law is fine by him; and besides, he's got his own obsessional war to carry on. In addition, he's rarely seen as essential to Mother's psyche as his wife is.

If, however, Mother is very close to her father, then there's trouble ahead for sure, and Father's attempts to deal with this are going to demand some real flexibility. It's an ironical principle of coupling that a daughter who's been close to her father, with plenty of affirmative experience with him, has a harder time adjusting to the developmental and competence defects in her husband than one without that "good" background. In many instances, of course, her father has been showing off his wisdom and power for her for years and, accordingly, her young husband's immaturities and flaws shine through to her with wide-screen impact.

In marriages which feature her very visible father, the young husband faces an assortment of costly options. One is to lie down and play dead and hope that the long-range gains of money, goods or prestige from her father will somehow balance out the short-range losses in possession of her. Another is to fight her image of her father head on, although the chances of a clear-cut victory here are slim because her Dad's competence and flair still contrast so sharply with his own, still-developing capabilities. Her father has shown her so much of living that her husband's showing-off opportunities are severely diminished at the very outset. Another option is the relocation caper which, while troublesome and expensive, has an excellent track record of success. Many couples in these family circumstances can't ever get themselves together unless they move far away, and the New York husband has to find a reason to set up their home in Seattle, or vice versa. Of course that makes the in-law visits longer each time, but it's generally an acceptable part of the cost. Sometimes her father can still be quite a menace even at long range, and, in very vain men, the first ill-advised telephone complaint from daughter of some bad treatment by her husband will bring Dad in on the double, strutting and posing for his wife and daughter alike. These marriages used to be called annulments.

Next to Mother's mother, the other acceptable and usable relationship for either of them is Father's father. Like her father in the usual case, his father has a minimal interest in their marriage and almost never has any stake in seeing trouble arise. He has no great need for excessive contact with his son, and they generally get their personal business accomplished with a minimum of fuss: a ball game, a mutual repair job, a day of fishing, or what have you. Of all four parties in the parent-in-law game, his father is by all odds the most benign of the group, except, perhaps, when father and son are in business together. Thus it is a rare wife who has problems with her father-in-law, and often the relationship, as skimpy as it usually is, is a pure plus for both of them. Interestingly, both fathers can sometimes become outstanding grandfathers to the child, once removed from the Oedipal stresses which regulated them so much with their own children. This late-developing ability often leaves their own children, now grown, slightly dumbfounded and at a loss for explanation; must be he's mellowed with age.

His mother, on the other hand, is a true emotional expatriate, and from her position in exile she watches their connection with brooding restraint and anxious ambivalence. Because she's an approval seeker, she must show all the outward signs of acceptance and contentment with their union and cannot even make jokes about her position for fear they would betray the ferment beneath. While her connection with her husband is a vital factor here, of course, she has, in addition, absorbed a couple of objectively heavy blows. No, she is not that often jealous of her daughter-in-law as some would have it, but as his mother she has had to accept the open and sometimes bitter demotion at the hands of the young wife's mother to Mother Number Two, or, as the grandchildren will later put it, "my other grandma." Her awareness that she has been busted in rank by their marriage seldom dissipates entirely, and it represents a legitimate setback to her own approval-seeking needs.

Then too, her own son deals her a wicked shot with no apparent intent to do so. Her beautiful son, after some twenty odd years of closeness, however agitated, often connects with his wife with such abruptness and completeness, leaving his mother with withdrawal symptoms close to mourning, that she has to face cold turkey. He's just gone, and in many cases his mother is left with some bad feelings, not that she lost him to his wife, but purely from the feelings of rejection and loss his total departure has produced.

Sometimes, married Sonny ropes his mother back into his life, and his apparent devotion to his Mom becomes a major weapon in his struggle with his wife. Called a "Mama's boy" by his wife, Sonny adroitly maneuvers himself between the two of them, and his mother can be a powerful punishing agent in the heavy in-fighting of attention getting. If his father-in-law is one of those vivid and charismatic chaps mentioned above, in the head-on struggle his mother becomes the only blade sharp enough to draw blood from his wife.

In most situations, therefore, Mother's mother becomes the significant in-law, often formidable, as Father and Mother go about building their family life. Grandmother obviously becomes a major attention-getting rival to Father, but his difficulties with her are not nearly as consistent as the countless jokes of night-club comics would imply. As he always does, Father surveys the situation and arranges his reaction repertoire accordingly, depending on how strong his position seems with Mother. There are situations, as noted earlier, where Father will pull

Mother entirely away from her mother and family if it can be managed, usually by pouring gasoline on the smoldering flames of perpetual animosities between Mother and one or both parents. If the parties involved are the types who literally won't speak to each other for long periods of time in pique, then the job is made simpler and is often accomplished with dispatch. But Father usually accomodates his mother-in-law, sometimes for services rendered, mostly out of pure necessity when he sees her emotional clout with her daughter, and sometimes because his mother-in-law is simply a first-class human being, caring, helpful and fair. Predictably, we have no technical or jargon term for a first-class human being, but there are many out there, and his mother-in-law is often one of them.

And generally Mother's connection to her mother is visibly strong, so that Father reorganizes his possessive strategies, which often includes some overt advantages to him directly from Grandmother. He notices, for example, that Mother, in true approval-seeking tradition, is subtly intimidated by her own mother, and preparations for a visit from Grandmother often include unconscious little touches and frills of care and tension not found at other times with other people. Mother will often insist on her "closeness" to her mother at all times and is legitimately downcast if she has to admit that maybe her need to please her has a few elements of fear in it. "Just habit, I guess. It doesn't really mean anything."

Her mother's help with the child often becomes extensive, even when on-premises time for Grandmother is limited. If they are in easy telephone range, the calls can exceed daily frequency, and Mother is usually able to acknowledge Grandmother's expertise in child matters, at least in the beginning, without feeling the fool. Her mother often becomes her adviser on the child, and the showing-off benefits for Grandmother should be obvious. It is Mother's anxiety about the first child which opens the door for the increasingly close connection between the two, although the door is later slammed shut when some of the competitive stresses involving all parties become a little sticky.

Mother ends up assessing her own growth and maturity by the degree of her dependency on her own mother. In exceptional cases, in order to get Mother in the first place, Father had to accept Grandmother, sometimes in the same house, right from the beginning.

Grandmother's value as chief baby sitter and surrogate Spock itself becomes a consideration of the first rank. If Mother can leave the child safely with Grandmother, she's an infinitely better companion for Father than if the child is temporarily watched over by a teenaged hired hand. Grandmother herself has to make some complex decisions about just how much attention she should pay to the grandchild, and at what times. Grandfather will often have an attack of the moodies if Grandchild is around too much, and he can make life unpleasant for his wife at such times, just like the good old days and for the same reasons. His daughter and son-in-law often have no idea that their child causes such problems.

In the current era of single-parent homes, Grandmother has come in for some very heavy play. His mother, and hers, are often pressed into service when the trouble breaks out, and for young children Grandma becomes a sensitive part of their support system. For many of these children, their Grandmother becomes the most consistent and stable person in the environment, and for some of them Grandmother becomes their mother. Married or single, Mother feels a whole lot better with her child at Grandma's because with her, the child not only gets expertise but affection as well.

On that score Grandmother is often the emotional jackpot for many children, a truly unique individual. Grandmother's version of "common sense" sometimes shows her to be a smart older woman who has learned from her life experiences and has gained perspective on some of the pitfalls of approval seeking when applied to children. She realizes that much of her own young motherhood was wasted on nonsense and expectations, hounding and criticizing others in the family about a lot of things that didn't really matter anyway, and she has now reached, in a sense, her full maturity as a human being. The result of this learning is that Grandmother can give the child something it can get from no other source: nonstop approval without cost or performance from the child. She has now satisfied herself that when all the pretentious techniques and hollow philosophies are stripped away, a child is truly a wonder of life and is best appreciated as such without all the anxious posing and thunderous display she once thought so necessary in the pursuit of approval goals.

If he can ever resolve his competitive stresses, Father himself may be lucky enough to have one such person in his life, one who can give him what Grandmother gives his child, and that is his daughter. No wife, son, mother, father, lover or mistress can perform this miracle of relationship: approval and admiration for the doing of absolutely nothing. Father's girl can invest him with the robes of the true hero, and the sole *quid pro quo* is that he merely show up. Everywhere else Father goes, he has to earn his way for love, respect, money or whatever. Only his daughter gives her rewards to him for free, and if left to her own devices will continue that way until mid-teen time, when she has to leave him for her own growth purposes.

Grandmother's term of office with the child is roughly ten or eleven years, at which time the child will become immersed with peers and peer values, so abhorred by America's control-conscious society. But during her time, Grandmother will perform her singular wonders for the child, and, of course, picking up plenty of approval for herself along the way. Mother and Father have some very testy reactions after the child has had an especially long stay with Grandmother. The child has been terribly "spoiled," they say, and now they have to devote time and energy to straightening him out, which means that Grandmother has asked nothing obvious in return for all her approval, and the kid has some temporarily uppity feelings about his own personal worth. Sometimes Grandmother and the child's parents get carried away with the competition, and some nasty scenes erupt about the right way to care for a child. Father's position in these bouts varies, as always, depending on his attention level from Mother. Sometimes he sides with Mother against Grandmother and will make a spirited speech or two denouncing Grandmother's competitive needs to be the matriarch; at other times he will apparently side with Grandma and attack Mother for letting her get so damned involved with the child in the first place.

If Mother and Father split up and, as is sometimes the case, the child is given to Grandmother to raise, she can generally be counted on to do an excellent job. The child gets all that approval and can show off for Grandmother in a way that Mother and Father might never allow. If society were all that concerned about the welfare of troubled children who effectively become wards of the bureaucracy, they would turn most of them over *pronto* to a selected Grandmother for the balance of their years of dependency, and half the child's troubles would be diminished within thirty days.

Instead, in such cases one has to listen to interminable discussions of mother figures, father figures, male roles and the assorted exotica of faddishness from the social work professionals and court hacks whose child placements have become legend for their accuracy and "appropriateness." Grandmothers of the type described above could do the job in spades if ever given the opportunity. Ah well, that would be a "simplistic" solution to a terribly complex problem; wouldn't the boys all turn out homosexual, and wouldn't the girls be hopelessly out of step with their peers? That the problems of living for many such troubled children are often quite simple to "cure" is an admission that a credentially rigid society cannot afford to make.

Whatever her objective virtues and vices, Father generally finds a way to live with Mother's mother as a major competitor. Over the long haul his position about his mother-in-law will fluctuate, as does his position about most other things in his life, depending on the current readings of the attention meter. The essential variability of his behavior does not mean that he lacks some strong feelings about the events and people around which he varies his actions. Father certainly does have those feelings, and two of these areas are worth extended discussion: his work and his child all by itself.

5

Life with Father

Father usually has trouble living the balanced life that Mother can manage. Whatever it is that has Father occupied, from the boardroom to the bowling alley, his mental eye forever roams to the grandstand to check if the woman seated in Section One has her attention on him. Father finds it difficult to achieve balance under the best of circumstances, and feelings of greater or lesser intensity than he *should* express are promptly and consistently discouraged. Except, that is, in apparent involvement with the children, where the experts routinely encourage Father to become more "involved" with his kids; excess about children and their affairs seems always legitimate in America.

When Father is heavily into a career and the challenges and emotional rewards it often promises, he discovers anew that there is a diagnostician around every corner just waiting to nail him for all that excess. "Workaholic" is today's chic jive for some men, meaning that Father is a work junkie because he's so damned spiritually empty elsewhere. Those who look at life from the balance view have Father coming and going as usual, and any expression of imbalance is easily spotted and diagnosed. Once having given Father's excess a name, the experts seem to rest easier, content now that in any discussion with Mother about working, Father will start out behind, disoriented by the diagnosis.

But deviation from balance works in both directions, and when considering his direct and personal feelings about his child, Father's world now finds him coming up short rather than long. Yes, indeed, Father has feelings about the child, but generally they don't seem strong enough to the media health experts. It seems right from the start that Father's intensity of feeling about the child doesn't reach Mother's, although there are some stories these days of a few fathers who nurture the child rather well. But these stories, by their very publicity, seem only to show what Father *might* do if he had a mind to. And look at those millions of divorced fathers, the "Sunday fathers," who see the kids once a week, buy a few toys, and then, naturally, are accused of "buying the children's love." Isn't that perfect proof that their feelings are just not there the way they *should* be?

These days, we are told, fathers are being granted custody of their children more and more often. Doesn't that indicate some basic changes in society? Not very likely. Father seldom sues for custody because he does not see himself as the expert on mothering in the way that Mother sees herself as the expert on fathering. Accordingly, he recognizes that the kids prefer living with Mother and that there's nothing wrong about that. Mother will only lose custody or be demoted to joint custody if she suffers from a very visible disability, like intermittent hospitalization, or if there is a substantial part of her that wants to lose, so that Father's "victory" is a real relief to her. For Father to sue Mother for custody, he has to be irrationally angry with her, usually about her new man, or he has to believe that the kids would be better off without her, which he rarely does. The society still finds it hard to believe that men and women are often different in feelings and objectives and that Father and Mother do not think alike. And the judges still come from political clubhouses, not from Athens or Sparta.

It's a critical land for Father these days, and because the critics are often coming from different directions than he is, Father is angry and disgusted with his inability to get a fair hearing. Father has enough troubles in his work, which used to be considered the very core of the "man's world," to last him a good long time. Let's look in at Father as he goes to work in search of satisfactions and rewards which help to define his personal destiny and which often have vital implications for his life at home.

Father Goes To Work

It has been held by some that Father's job is his mistress, and his love for his work makes the job a linear and almost sexual rival of Mother's. While that is sometimes true when Father is actually out there working, it is almost never true when he's at home with Mother and the kids. When he's home, Father's job is *his* child and is generally presented with the same objectives in mind that Mother has when she talks of *her* child, the flesh-and-blood one. The goal for both of them is to keep each other and the kids on notice that the job each holds is so hard and so exhausting that fatigue is his or her constant companion and that anyone who doesn't appreciate that fact is only a fraction above a savage.

Mother's version of Calvary, the kids, is amply supported by middle-class society which never tires of telling itself that parenting is the most difficult job in the world. Every superlative of agony and effort is expended on an everyday basis, as we shall see, and the objective is clear at one hundred paces: the raising of children is hell on wheels for a woman, and she is well within her rights to be "all in" at the end of the day. The effort-vendors for women, of course, are also usually offering a course or two on how to make it more successful, but even when it is made so, parenting is still the most arduous work ever invented. The job of trying to develop all that potential in the kids is incurably difficult.

Father falls into his male version of the verb "to suffer" for obvious attention-getting reasons, but from other causes as well. The famous Puritan work ethic which held that hard work was practically and spiritually essential for any kind of progress is retranslated for emotional use to mean that any eight hours of work, whatever it is, is hard, regardless of the progress, if any. Any father who tosses off a remark about how easy his job is and what little effort it requires is either drifting unconsciously toward a breakdown or is a ne'er-do-well who probably steals the Company blind anyway.

When Father uses his work to solicit sympathy from Mother and the kids, he's as close as he can get to the approval-seeker's martyrdom. Unfortunately, martyrdom is a relatively chronic condition, so if he is into it by the age of thirty-five, some aspects of the future are predictable. When both Mother and Father are simultaneously committed to the sympathy caper through their respective persecutors, the kids and the job, then the children have a daily running of the Misery Derby at the dinner table, with each course bringing fresh new moans and complaints. Many children scarcely remember a meal without their parents at a constant whine, so that the kids can't even get in a complaint about school, each other or even the dog. After dinner the kids are expected to do homework at hours which would being self-righteous cries for overtime from either of the parents in that environment.

The pleas for sympathy for the overwhelming fatigue have no relation to the personalities of the men or the types of jobs involved and nothing to do with the objective level of difficulty. The laziest of men, doing the least difficult work, can seek sympathy with the same desperate enthusiasm as men completely absorbed in truly draining tasks, it makes no difference. Consistent with the suffering theme, both Mother and Father are soliciting old-fashioned, approval-type appreciation from each other and the kids, and the atmosphere of weariness and guilt in the family could be cut with a butter knife. To improve the effect, one or both will take to sleeping "from exhaustion," so for the kids the overall impact is to give their home a strangely crypt-like feel, where one walks softly through the scattered bodies.

When simple sympathy and appreciation are not forthcoming, the male remedy of the past has been to raise the ante with threats of poor health brought on by "pressure" at the job. Actually, there is some question as to which comes first, the sympathy or the poor health. What's pressure? It means whatever forces can produce acute anxiety, especially concerning the making of mistakes, getting a task done by a time deadline, or making poor decisions. Ask any man if he works under much pressure, and it's the rare fellow who says, "No, not really. There's some occasionally, but it doesn't bother me" – especially if Mother is within earshot.

A decade or two ago the disease which threatened literally to eat up the male population was ulcers. Yes, the research clearly showed that persons in decision-making capacities, especially those who internalized their feelings and didn't let out their anxieties, were very prone to developing ulcers. And ulcers meant trouble: special diets, sporadic and spontaneous pains which bent a man in two, right over the dinner table. Did the ulcers hurt? Certainly. Ask anybody who actually has one, though you'll have to search a bit before finding one. Once the diagnosis was formulated and popularized, fathers everywhere had one or were developing one. A national panic was on, and health leaders gave their pedantic views on the competitive stresses eating away at Father's gut and the price men pay for success. Sounds incredible, now that ulcers have been abolished so quickly. The cure was simple enough. The disease just didn't do the job, so another, more frightening one was clearly needed. Ulcers were just too damned pedestrian to work that well, and besides, Mother didn't seem all that impressed with the special diets. Ulcers were eliminated by gentlemen's agreement.

To take its place and to do a better all-around job of attention getting, heart attacks and "heart conditions" were polished up and presented as the "in" diagnosis. Some twenty years later, the same speeches, the same admonitions, the same cultural warnings once made about ulcers are issued about heart conditions, and still for the same purpose. A plethora of books and articles has appeared over the years identifying the most likely victims, giving the latest pointers on avoiding this dangerous disease and giving the family advice on how to help Father relax and unwind after a pressured and stressful day. The jackpot here, of course, is that heart conditions can kill, fast, which ulcers simply couldn't do. Ulcers could bore Mother to death faster than they could bleed Father.

The physician's explanation for giving Father the heart diagnosis is plain common sense. Father gets dizzy, or even hits the deck at home, and at the emergency room they can't find a thing. The doctor surveys his patient, and he looks like a man in search of something. Rather than have Father have to go to the trouble of hitting the deck again two months later, he is given what he needs – the diagnosis of a "mild heart condition," which only shows up on the EKG on Wednesday mornings at two. Immoral? Hardly, since the recipient of the diagnosis is openly relieved and damned happy to have such a good diagnostician at his side.

The actual cardiac terrors from stress are pretty much of the same theme as ulcers, but the purpose of it, to gain attention by scaring others close to you, is where the money is. Health certainly has its uses, especially if it is bad or alleged to be bad. There are those who wonder today how it can be that suddenly almost every substance and every human activity is found to be a possible cause of cancer, and the answer is in the payoff coming to researchers who discover something "new." The government does not give grant funds for negative results, so the sky's the limit on cancer. In another ten years, when the cardiac-stress business is exposed for the deception it generally is, Father will either have to invent an even more terrifying syndrome to scare Mother, like Spontaneous Brain Disintegration, or will have finally to admit that, in fact, he generally likes to work and that his suffering there has been a different kind of lie all along.

Father has a fairly good time at work. He's often seriously challenged by his job, and he usually has a whole cast of people at the job who provide some interest, even sometimes some fun. It's much like a game, where there are winners and losers, depending on an array of skills and strengths, and there is generally a certain excitement to it interspersed with some stretches of boredom and anxiety. It's a lot like a football game, and the jock language so relished in corporate offices indicates the similarities. This is the "male model of achievement" the books speak of, even though the children seldom ever get a peek at Dad when he's out achieving, only when he's home complaining to Mother.

Father does believe that working should be hard; otherwise, how else could you tell the difference between working and playing, except for the money? The competition, of course. Father spends his day among acquaintances and sometimes friends, but generally they are competitors. And if Father doesn't have a need to beat the competitors, then he's not ambitious in the conventional sense. Thus, the work has to be difficult in the very doing in order to inflate the value of future rewards. On a purely abstract basis, there are fathers who still gag on the belief that in their view, their child's life today is so easy. They have some serious temper problems around the notion that if people aren't sweating, literally or otherwise, there's something wrong somewhere.

Father's belief that work should be hard gets him into all kinds of problems in his career. His need to see himself as a hard worker often causes him to misread his own ambitions, to mistake conscientious and diligent effort for ambition in the beat-out-the-other-guys sense. The first is essential to some degree for the second to flow upward, but hard work alone will not put Father at the top of the heap. Achievement really refers to the first entity, indicating a person who does work hard and can persevere at his task, but who also feels the challenge of excellence, of doing it right. Ambition, on the other hand, refers to some degree of the achieving need, but more than that alone, to an eye for its competitive uses when aggressively dealing with others. The ambitious ones have always a bit of achievement in them, but the achieving ones may or may not be ambitious.

The workaholic diagnosis, actually intended to wound rather than enlighten, covers many such men, among others. Interestingly, the original workaholics in organizations were often women rather than men. Career executive secretaries have toiled for years with enormous capabilities, a disregard for time and its limits, and utterly responsive to the challenge of getting it done right. Their reward was to be pitied rather than pilloried for living their lives for the Company, and sometimes they were leered at for what many felt must be an inordinate sexual attraction to the long-time Boss. These women, possessed of staggering levels of conscientiousness and responsibility, had little ambition and were content to stay in their assisting roles, with Father as the Boss. Father reciprocated his deep regard for his secretary by ignoring the advantages of the dictating machine and continuing to use the now peculiar practice of stenography, where he gets to show off his wisdom and power for her and she scribbles his every word into her book. Often the executive secretary ends up with Father's checkbook, indicating that Mother is the child of the pair, and Father is in need of some oblique nurturing.

Many fathers in the same psychological position are snared by the workaholic diagnosis. They maintain incredible hours on the premises to control their own anxieties and guilts, which would come from relaxing and doing nothing, still believing that this means they are ambitious and right-thinking. Their disappointments later, when the promotions go to other men, often less capable ones at a particular task but more involved in scanning the environment for opportunity, embitter them somewhat, but generally not enough to make them swear off the long hours. Of course, the workaholic label is often applied to a number of fathers who are by no means this conscientious type. One fairly large group of diagnosees is out having a good time elsewhere, usually with another woman, and Father in this case is rather pleased to be a workaholic in Mother's eyes, since it obscures all manner of sins and alternative mini-life styles. There's a second huge group, however, of fathers who are actually on the premises, but not really doing much of anything after hours, except passing time and making Mother wait at home, thereby maintaining himself as the center of some anguished and agitated attention.

Now that Mother is seriously getting into careers for herself, she's going to meet at first hand the conscientiousness/ambition dilemma which often confuses Father. Mother is going to have to examine the extent of her ambitions, and it isn't going to be easy. Half a lifetime of approval seeking will make the line between working hard and real ambition extremely hazy, as it often is for Father, with predictably negative results. Solid and consistent effort is always recognized out there, but there is little overt reward simply because the ambitious ones are generally competing for the same prizes, but with a more widely stocked arsenal. Some get to be President, and others get a gold watch.

The Case of the Working Mother has been one of the sorrier chapters in psychological studies for some time now. Ever since the fifties, the working mother has been a top contender for the annual Evil of the Year prize the social scientists seem always to be awarding to one disaster or another. The original theme was simple enough: when Mother went to work, for whatever reason, and was not at home at three o'clock when Sonny and Sis returned from school, the unsupervised children, in their rage at her absence, set immediately to antisocial behavior, with Sonny resolved to set fire to an old man and Sis skipping down the block for a gang bang. As usual, how this dynamic actually might work was never made clear, but all that matters is that the diagnosis was made, and the bad guys were named – sort of like cops and robbers.

It certainly worked on Mother. What was produced was a group of working women, defensive and timid, who claimed they were working "just to help out," "to make a little extra," or "for vacation money," rather than being able to say they worked because they wanted to or because they badly needed to get out of the house. In those days, Mother showed any real ambition only at her peril and, like Father today, was often reluctant to acknowledge the fact that working could be fun and that she enjoyed it. Father then and now would often get his pound of flesh from her anyway by making it difficult for her to accomplish if he didn't want her to work, or by making her account for every penny of her money if he did, or, as was more usual, if he was ambivalent about the whole thing. When he isn't making things difficult for her to test how tough she is, Father generally treats his working wife pretty well because her being out in the world has his alarm system ringing, and his desire to hold on to her regains top priority for the most part.

Since Mother generally is still not allowed to be sick, there is no chance of her erecting a health myth to match Father's ulcers and cardiac arrests. Mother is allowed to develop cancer, but that can't be easily related to working, so is of little value here. What career-minded Mother does today is to counter with the only feasible-sounding protective myth she has handy, namely, that the men discriminate against her because she's a woman, thereby holding her back. The implication is that Mother is bursting with ambition, and that the poor treatment given her by some men demonstrates that by its very existence. Mother would be well off indeed if that were her biggest worry. That some men out there will disparage her efforts and undermine her confidence puts her exactly equal with Father.

There's no approval to be had in any serious career, because that world is infested with competitors who do not wish you well and who are hoping to profit from your mistakes. When either Mother or Father complains about bad people trying to hold them back, and if the world were really fair they'd have reached the top by now, one wonders if the speaker understands ambition and competition and the price one must necessarily pay in order to have even a shot at winning the game. "Fair" is not what the game is about.

Father has long been used to the fact that if he does have ambitions he needs to satisfy, there is a certain amount of humiliation he will have to accept along the way in any kind of vertical structure with a chain of "bosses." Father can't really complain about it very seriously because his own ambitions have placed him in these situations, and he generally realizes that heavy complaining about it on the job is tantamount to saying, "Why won't you all make it easier for me? Can't you see I'm a worthy fellow who, if I had no competitors, would do such a fine job?" Some of the humiliation is simply in the chemistry, as when a man above him takes a dislike to Father and makes damned sure he doesn't get that promotion, in which case Father often has to leave that group and look elsewhere. Another part of the humiliation is more tied up with the vertical structure, where Father feels to some extent compelled to render little nuances of subjugation, generally classified under the generic title of ass-kissing. A certain amount of this is going to be done over the years, unless Father fancies himself as a "maverick," which means a man who shows off his courage in the very teeth of the establishment by getting strategically fired and living off his heralded potential for years.

Perhaps the limiting case of confusion surrounding ambition, conscientiousness, and the price to pay for either, is found in those situations where Father decides to give Sonny the business, sometimes literally. Does Father want the family business to pass to his children so that they'll have a stake in the world or a head start with their peers? Yes he does, but his motive is seldom as purely altruistic in nature as it appears to some. Whenever Sonny or son-in-law decides to come into the business with Father, it is inherently a test of Sonny's aspirations and desire to create something on his own. Father, past his acknowledged good intentions in showing off for Mother, has confessed that he has some doubts as to how well the kids can cut it on their own. They don't seem as tough or as sharp as he is himself; perhaps taking them into the business is the only human thing to do. Mother is comforted in her apprehensions for the kids and will to some degree accept Father's largesse in the name of the children, while acknowledging Father's stardom. Sonny, however, is often wary of Father and the business, sometimes because his interests and ambitions legitimately go elsewhere, and sometimes because something inside him tells him to watch out.

When Father does get to give Sonny or Sis's husband the business, he does it in one of two ways. In the first, Sonny joins a going concern, where Father has been doing just about everything himself for years and is not about to change that. Sonny accepts his titular status with varying amounts of gratitude or guilt and usually with little if any ambition of his own showing. While Father is alive, Sonny profits along with him, generally envied by his peers for having it made. If Father is vindictive and hasn't gotten his due from Mother for what he did for the kids, then he lets Sonny do nothing important and learn nothing at all. Sure enough, two years after Father's death Sonny is found, aged forty-one, in the Federal Bankruptcy Court. Sonny stands, dejected and defeated, not at all clear about what happened. He had mistaken Father's ambition for his own, and even his conscientiousness wasn't sufficient to teach him that the name of the game is to make money.

In the second case, Sonny survives because he has ambition at least sufficient to make him question Father's judgment and to cause a fairly chronic level of disagreement and unpleasantness between the two of them. The arguments and unpleasantness are the price he has to pay for his ambition, because unlike the first instance, his needs will not allow him to lie down and play dead in the face of Father's superior experience and wisdom. He can't simply take the money from Father, as in the case above, getting along wonderfully well with everybody, while his own fate is being sealed daily amidst the good fellowship. Even then, assertive, surviving Sonny still wonders about himself and whether he could have done it on his own, as he knows his peers have similarly suspected about him.

In short, conscientiousness makes an excellent worker and generally endears him to others because he can be counted upon to produce responsibly and consistently. Ambition, on the other hand, doesn't produce much approval because the ambitious one is always looking for ways to manipulate the environment, including most of the people in it. Conscientiousness speaks for itself, without interpretation, in the quantity and quality of the work product; ambition has to be presented to others with some care, otherwise the reflex fear and anger it generates will often demolish the very purpose of it. A great deal of Father's personal destiny depends on how well he reads his own needs on this score and how much of a price he's willing to pay in striving to win the competitive struggle with the other guys.

If Father is conscientious and not ambitious, it generally means that he wants to do the job right and, in the approval-seeking sense, he'll need some appreciation and maybe even a few friends, just like Mother. If Father is somewhat conscientious, but ambitious as well, close friendships play little part in his plan, and his need to show off at home will flame visibly, albeit intermittently, amidst the attention-getting pattern with Mother and the kids. In either case, Father is dead serious in his feelings about his work when he's out there, although his level of enjoyment of it, even excitement in it, is considerably higher than his symptoms at home would ever suggest.

For her part, career-minded Mother is taking no chances. Researchers, themselves usually ardent sisters, now repeat with timely assurance that women are really afraid of success because the culture has threatened them with rejection by men if they should shine too brightly. Fear of success will accomplish for Mother in her career what "potential" has done for Father in his; it allows one to fail or lose on the merits, yet still talk animatedly about what might have been. Not bad.

Father Alone With His Child

The other area of his life where Father has some very definite feelings concerns his child. Yes, Father has some strong feelings about the child quite unto himself, even though what he will show later on often reflects the current state of his feelings about Mother and the competitive, attention-getting stresses in the family. Father is often urged these days to pitch in and share in the doing of child-care chores, seemingly on the assumption that his domestic labors would be direct evidence of his feelings for the child. When he comes up short, as he usually does, the masculine-sex-role-stereotype-argument button is pressed, as reviewed earlier. The baby, however, is hers, out of her body, not his, and no matter how hard Father has tried spiritually and physically to lodge himself in Mother's viscera, the connection between the child and Mother is not to be duplicated.

Indeed, Father can manage to get himself into big trouble when he tries to argue and demonstrate that his feelings for the child are the same as Mother's. The thrust of such an argument is similar to trying to prove oneself innocent in Court, with predictably absurd results. In rare instances, which the media devour hungrily, Father throws himself into it with a fury, takes off a year from work and gives the baby two mothers for the price of one. The couple in question report enormous emotional benefits to each other, and, of course, are to be envied for that. What advantages there are to the child remain to be seen.

Father's sensitivity to the accusations that he has no feelings for the child, especially a very young child, when his feelings are really just *different* from Mother's, of a lower order in intensity, pride and range, gets Father into some foolish debate. It causes him almost unconsciously to equate an admission that his feelings are different with a confession of not caring at all, which he knows isn't really so. But Mother is often convinced that her standards of feeling are the *only* healthy standards, rather than merely the mother's standards. Reality will continue to feature two sexes until further notice.

Father reports, for example, that he rather enjoys watching the child in its crib while it sleeps. What's Father feeling? Many things, apparently, from affectionate curiosity to some psyching himself up for the next day's work by gazing down at his help-less dependent and soaking up some strength. Interestingly, Father often prefers these silent moments alone, without Mother around. Some of that desire for solitude is connected to the romantic stress with Mother, and Father sometimes reports that his crib-gazing was hastily interrupted by the sound of Mother's step, which provokes him to retreat into the next room so as not to be found mooning over the child. Yes, the baby has been identified as hers all right, and the identification will trickle into some deep corners. But some of Father's desire to do his child-mooning alone stems from another major source. The following report by a young father of twenty-six captures it with uncommon eloquence.

> I used to like to sit next to her crib and watch her. When she slept, I'd sometimes put my ear to her chest and listen to her heart beat. Scared the hell out of me – she's really alive. That little thump sound in her chest used to seem so weak to me. The whole thing was too much. Everytime I'd go near the crib when her mother was home, she'd want me to do something – pick her up, hold her, take her for a walk in the stroller.

Mother's desire to have Father emulate her own showing-off activities with the child summarizes perfectly the problems they have over the fact that they are different people. Mother used to rage, in fact, that Father would seldom be interested in taking the child for a promenade around the neighborhood in the stroller. Originally, Father was seen as selfish and uncooperative, but more sophisticated interpretations had it that Father was weak on public strollering because he was afraid his masculine image would suffer irreparable damage. Neither was generally the case; strollering the child was Mother's showing-off activity, but not Father's. Yet the current cultural need to diagnose the difference in preference, rather than accept it for what it is, simply a difference of no great significance, is typical and consta it.

Father simply doesn't have that many showing-off activities with children, or certainly nowhere near as many as Mother has, and it is this difference that is diagnosed by Mother and others as substandard behavior by Father. This is especially true when the child is quite young, say less than ten. Later on, if the child demonstrates some unusual talent or skill, then Father sometimes gets into showing off about his child. This special skill is usually athletic, or less frequently, academic achievement, but in either case, when these fathers get to showing off, one wonders if the children in question would have been better off with some good old-fashioned neglect.

Actually, Father's natural stance with his young child seems strikingly similar to the behavior of the male parent in the higher-order primate families in captivity or in the wild. When a gorilla, chimpanzee or rhesus monkey baby arrives and is allowed to grow a little, it spends most of its time with its mother. Since the primate baby suckles from its mother, there's no doubt in its mind where it belongs. If it has access to Father, it will occasionally wander over to him to play. Father sits, glowering at onlookers and thinking his thoughts. He looks down at the baby as it begins to fool with him and suffers it patiently until the baby's antics become too bothersome, then cuffs it softly away. The baby returns to mother for grooming and other play as well as for sleep.

But when the primate father has to care for the baby, for reasons natural or experimental, he does so, but with a diligence and attention to detail that is clearly below mother's. He grooms the baby somewhat carelessly, he plays with the baby, but not very systematically, he looks at the baby, but only intermittently, but he does the job at least to Darwinian satisfaction for the child's purposes, even if his performance might not earn kudos from the organization of female primates. In the primates, Father protects those in the cage with him, as one learns quickly if one decides to go near the infant.

Well, certainly we have come a long way past the apes, haven't we? We certainly have a right to expect more parenting from Father than mere protection. But such blithe assumptions may be mistaken. Anyone who thinks the job of protecting the child *is* being done had best look again, for perhaps the soaring standards of today's parenting may have taken Father right past his primary business into trivia and absurdity.

Father does get his chance sometimes to take care of the kids. All fathers do from time to time when Mother gets sick and can't function. During these intermittent episodes, Father discovers the other side of the coin is also heads: housework simply sits and looks back at you, without beginning or end, laundry has a life of its own, unkillable by any means, and the constancy of food preparation and cleaning up adds its own timeless quality to the scene, which, despite the effort and energy, seems always the same, day after day. When Mother recovers and is back on the job, these short bouts for Father serve merely to educate him briefly and set his temper to grinding. But other fathers, a relative few, get a real chance to do it nonstop when there is a more chronic collapse within the family.

The Negligent Mother

There is a certain small percentage of marriages wherein Father becomes Mother for most practical purposes. The term "negligent," of course, is a purely relative one, but for our purposes it refers to a mother's inability to perform with any degree of consistency the basic functional tasks which normally are her lot. The quality of the doing of such tasks is a secondary matter, since children are much more tied in to constancy of service than excellence. Nor does negligent in this case mean much in the emotional area either, since these children generally feel loved sufficiently; they are just short on the practical side of being cared for.

Mother in such cases is usually a severely narcissistic woman who has found child-rearing simply too much for her in just about every respect. She feels she can't keep up with even one child, and the household very early begins its schedule where nothing is done when it is supposed to be done. Chores like shopping and laundry become especially vexing, and the empty refrigerator soon becomes as much of a symbol of this version of collapse as the mounds of dirty laundry and the children's inquiries for a favorite garment.

Mother feels herself overwhelmed not only by what appear to

be insurmountable obstacles of chores and duties, but also by the chill brought on by the apparent end of her own childhood, when she has to step aside and care for others. Her usual resolution is to sleep nearly all the time, and the children become accustomed to approaching her for one request or another when she is in a prone position. Mornings and late afternoons are simply too hard for her to navigate; her fatigue is incurable. Periodically she will rouse herself to put in a few good days, as when Grandmother comes for a visit, but these intervals are seldom very predictable in advance.

Her problem, a fair number of times, is aggravated or soothed, whichever, by a mild but chronic alcohol habit, which generally allows her to return to her bed feeling a bit more justified in her little nap, or perhaps to stimulate a few fantasies from better days now gone forever. Her behavior in the house has now established her as one of the permanent party of children, and probably number-one at that. Her alcohol intake is not sufficient to put her on the kitchen floor, as in legitimate alcoholism; it's simply enough to have it noticed constantly, and before they are very old the kids are making allowances for it.

Father in such situations often begins a gradual transformation into a kind of hybrid parent where, whatever his sex role might be, his practical role broadens ever wider in range. The first chores he takes over on his own are cooking and laundry because these are not postponeable activities. After years of cooking Father will sometimes become quite adept at it, but in most cases it remains adequate and nothing more. Excellence is not an integral part of the bargain. Getting the children fed and out in the morning soon has him altering the wake-up schedule or even his hours at work through an understanding boss.

At the end of his working day, Father again tries his best to cut corners so that he can get "back," as it is called, as soon as possible. He will often enlist the aid of other people, like his child's friend's mother, to keep the kids around for an hour or two, and a great deal of life takes on this jerry-built quality which is sustained for years. Father has a full-time career in these cases which rather defies neat description and catchy titles. He's actually in the position of the working mother whose major awareness is of time and priority chores. All other things being equal, Father gets the entire job done well enough, as long as one is not looking for superlatives of achievement.

If Father is making some money, then he'll usually find a woman to take over cleaning and other maintenance chores to help him out, and the money necessary for her becomes a standard feature of his budget. Mother arouses a good deal of bad feeling from others, including the helper, since she usually chooses to stick around, rather than run off as seriously narcissistic men commonly do. Others often wonder in such cases how Father does it, or "puts up with it," and there are even those who would call him weak because he didn't toss her out years ago.

It's true, of course, that when Father is playing both pitcher and catcher he's frustrated and sometimes depressed at his inability to get any sustained attention from sleeping Mother. But in these situations Father has no competitors at all for her attention, not even the kids. She cares only about herself, and there just isn't anybody else out there, not him, the kids, nobody. She has, in addition, made it perfectly clear that she's more of a child than he is, so there's little point in competing with her on that score – the match has been a rout for years. And, if Mother is a pure narcissist, she has little if any hostility in her for anybody else, which makes compassion and forgiveness flow a lot more easily. She's not very angry at anybody; it's simply that she's the only one in the world.

Again, Father does an excellent job in these situations, at least when the standards applied to his efforts are apropos the circumstances. He's able to act pretty directly on the children's needs which include plenty of straight-out nurturing and other taking-care-of activities. Would he do all of this if it weren't forced on him by Mother's unusual disability? Probably not. His *desire* to do it at all would probably not count as very relevant to the children in question, since they are seldom concerned with the esthetics of parenting, at least not until teen time. Father's feelings for the kids are there, and they are his, sure enough; that the expression of his feelings about the kids often depends on the circumstances of life seems to be one of the basic factors which has earned him second place in the parenting race by those who compare him head-to-head with Mother.

There are other circumstances, very different than those just described, which bring Father's feelings out in a different, much harsher way. The narcissistic mother provides Father with no visible competitors, which makes her easier to deal with than she looks to outsiders. In other circumstances, however, there is a child who glitters for a mother, not narcissistic in any pure sense, who hungers for a little stardom herself in cases where Father is simply not able to give her the showing-off opportunities she so badly needs. As a consequence, Father's feelings for this child start to bend and finally emerge, oblique but ugly, at least to the child and sometimes to Mother and child both.

The Apple of Her Eye

At the polar opposite of the situation just described lies a life circumstance more common than the negligent mother and one which summarizes the competitive dynamics of Father's life more clearly than any other. These are the situations where Mother seems to have found her true love, and it is not Father or any other man; it is Sonny or Sis, and especially when the child has star quality of one type or another. This is the area of the "favorite child," uniformly denied by all parents, but well known to many children who have a perspective here that is difficult to challenge. The favorite child is seldom everybody's favorite, and it's awfully rare that he is Father's favorite if he is Mother's, and vice versa.

This is also "stage mother" country, where the image is immediately provoked of a determined, if frustrated, mother, dragging her favorite moppet from audition to audition, sucking up the vicarious sunshine wherever it falls. There are stage fathers as well, but these tend to be found in athletics when Sonny, or occasionally Sis, shows some real talent, and Father, equally frustrated, appoints himself coach-in-residence, "guiding" the child to ever greater accomplishment. The image in either case is of almost universal distaste for the parent involved because of the embarrassingly obvious emotional exploitation shown at all levels. While the child itself is often a casualty in such cases, whether because of cumulative anxiety or simply from the training in being a bit of a monster, the party of interest for our purposes is the other parent, the one not absorbing all of those tortured positive gains from the child.

The other parent is usually Father, but when it happens to Mother the initial dynamics are much the same. Father is in a perpetual state of exile as he watches Mother and her star-child swing down the lane of life together. If he has no appetite of his own for picking up the crumbs which dribble off the edges, then he will be unable to join the extravaganza, even as chauffeur or coat-holder. When Father does manage to join in the fun, as he sometimes does, then one is treated to a panoramic view of the monster family, all trading on the child's real or imagined capabilities.

From the vantage point of the child, he sees it always as a direct interest in him by either parent and can sometimes see their frustrated ambitions behind it all. As always, however, the child doesn't see the connection and interplay between the parents, which go a long way toward revealing the dynamics of their love affair. Furthermore, the child often sees the attention and guidance from the parent as good things for himself, even with the pressure they eventually provoke, and will often credit that attention with making a success of his life.

When Father takes a special interest in Sis, it is sometimes called the "mentor effect," meaning that he or some older man later on in her life saw her potential and was a critical force in helping to unleash it for achievement purposes. In earlier times, many women who achieved high academic or professional status were often able to credit their uncommon ambition to the encouragement and aid of an achieving father who had no qualms about challenging the cultural stereotypes facing his daughter. Mother was often described in more pedestrian terms, and the implication was that Mother was quite satisfied with Father's unusual involvement in Sis, except in extreme cases where some jealous friction flared openly.

Sis was seen also as a good subject for Father's aspirational interests because she was more willing than her brother to follow Father's career plans set down with such confidence. Sonny, being both less intimidated by Father and less anxious to please, often resisted Father's pushing in the same direction. Interestingly, Father's interest in Sis was usually interpreted as indicative of some mild inadequacy in the connection between him and Mother, grandly neglecting Father's use of Sis against Mother in their love struggle. Later, when talented Sis grows up and says that she always felt that Mother was a little jealous of her, the connotation is of Mother as something of a small person, but certainly not that Father was killing two birds with one stone. As always, the child sees Mother and Father as fixed quantities.

When it's Mother who's a bit over-invested in Sis, she seems to be pursuing pure approval-type goals with a minimum of interest in knocking Father about, although that is generally one of its effects. Whether Sis is good at music, art, baton-twirling or whatever, Mother gets herself out front solely for the joy of the public presentation of a winner, which brings about the satisfaction of others' envy and straight-out showing off. The admiration and envy she basks in are from the other women, but not men. Father, in such cases, is usually fighting the whole thing the way he typically does whenever Mother is too far into the kids. He claims that the child is "spoiled," and, as always, Father will dream up reasons for discipline, restrictions, curfews and other types of general harassment of the girl only recently invented. Whether he's punishing Mother or Sis is seldom clear to them because they've been long convinced that Father is simply moody and irascible.

The biggest disaster for Father, however, is when Mother connects with Sonny, the apple of her eye, with unusual intensity. In a recent survey of America's top professional comedians, for example, the family dynamic was revealed in flawless detail. Almost to a man, the most successful entertainers remembered their mothers as the ones who encouraged and supported them, who were audience, stage crew and public-relations apparatus all in one. They were seen as glistening children, sparkling with brains and aliveness, verbal as can be, with charm and aggressive presentation that would warm the coldest heart. What about Father? With striking unanimity again, Father was hostile to the son when at home, disinterested and often absent. Father made no effort to understand his son and his unique needs, nor did Father strive to take any active role in Sonny's life. In these unusual life conditions, Father was not only remote and indifferent, he was resentful and even scornful of his son and his ambition.

These latter terms, resentful and scornful, come very close to describing the counterattack which Father often launches against the child who is Mother's favorite, or any children, for that matter, when Father's competitive attention-getting fortunes are sagging at the hands of Sonny and Sis. Father does many things to Mother, as already reviewed, but to the kids themselves his revenge for his defeat often takes the form of an oblique hostility called "teasing," or what today would be called a "put-down."

Father Teases His Child: The Attack Begins

If, as Professor Freud suggested, humor can be a release for anxiety, then it must have been Mother he had in mind. Father's version of "fun" seems to spring from a different source when it's about the kids, and one would absolutely swear that it had something to do with anger. When Father is losing the obsessive struggle for Mother's mind, or when he's barely holding his own, he often gets very involved with fun, except that the kids seldom get the joke at any age. Father often accuses Mother of lacking a sense of humor, but the accusation is usually made after Mother has spent some time repairing the ego or the body of a crying child.

In the early stages, for example, as the eight-month-old infant struggles across the floor to grasp a ball which attracts it, Father may nudge the ball out of reach, just as the child approaches it. "Don't do that. Oh, that's mean," purrs Mother. "Oh, come on, now, I'm just playing with her, I'm just fooling," replies Father, again challenging Mother either to believe what she sees or believe his verbal interpretation of it. A few years later, Father is into roughhousing with little Sonny and, as so often happens, Sonny ends up crying after an especially energetic push from Father. Whoops, another accident. When Mother scolds Father for playing too rough with the child, Father counters by saying, "He likes it. Don't spoil a boy by treating him like a girl." Sure enough, Sonny usually keeps coming back for more, never sure if the roughhousing will end up being a playful physical romp or the other kind, where he lands on his head, "by accident." Mother believes that Father just doesn't realize his own strength, a most charitable view indeed.

Mother herself is not much of a teaser with the kids. The only consistent exception to this is when Sis has a weight problem, which Mother often shares with her, and Mother can get devilishly vicious, taunting Sis about her basic appeal to boys and her competitive deficits when compared with one or two of her friends. When pressed hard, Mother generally will lapse into straight-out criticism, and the goal of it is to minimize losses in approval generated by the kids. When long hair on boys first became common in the sixties, nearly all parents resisted vigorously, often aided and abetted by some strange school principals who a decade earlier were just as absorbed with the proper length of Sis's skirts. Mother criticized Sonny's hair as being not right and in poor taste for a boy, because in those days it was a sure approval-loser in the community. But Mother seldom went so far as Father's teasing of Sonny as a faggot, a "girl" who should at least get high heels to make his act complete.

When Father is a "great kidder" with the children, the range of subjects that he chooses to harass through jest is endless, and it's usually Sonny who is the target: the boy's strength, or lack of it; his size; his looks; his name; a pet name the child hates; his aspirations, when Sonny foolishly makes an especially grandiloquent statement of his life goals; his guts, of course; his dedication and perseverance in any project; his ambition relative to one of his friends; and, when the sap is really running, his brains. What makes Father's "kidding" so hard to deal with is that it is covert enough to allow a plea of innocence by Father when Mother confronts him with the almost-obvious, namely, that he's really very angry, and his teasing of the child is one very nasty habit. Father can still say, "Who, me?" and get away with it on a fair number of occasions.

The teasing is also almost always done at close-quarters and is seldom done out in the world where others may hear. It is one of those apparently hidden factors which bring such surprises later on, when everybody had thought it was the ideal family. There isn't much public teasing because that would bring some very obvious distaste and shock from others who accept things at face value rather than the joshing disclaimers. Sonny and Sis are always frustrated in responding to it because of its somewhat elusive nature and often grind their teeth in futility as Dad explains that he was just "having a little fun," and "can't you take a little joke?" If the teased child also happens to be the apple of Mother's eye, Father may even, in exceptional cases, select another child as his "favorite" for match play, with predictable results all around.

If Father's attack has been to taunt Sonny about how "tough" he is or how much "sacrifice" and "effort" he's willing to make to get ahead, Sonny is much inclined to bite the bullet on this one, causing him to make steady effort at tasks he no longer cares about. After a joyless senior year in high school, Sonny often goes off to college, where he drops out in a year or two because the whole thing doesn't make much sense to him any more. For some fathers, the teasing ploy represents a lifelong stance which helps make their grown children still uncertain about their feelings and motives. For other fathers, the teasing stops when the kid moves out into the world, and another developmental marvel is ascribed to "mellowing with age."

It is in the area of how smart Sonny or Sis is, or isn't, that the going gets tougher for the child, and Mother and Father come closer together in style. The teasing often fades into one of its close cousins, criticism, where Mother is at least the equal of Father, and the kids may move into an area of really heavy damage to their life forces. When the brightness and academic success of the kids is top-priority stuff, performed and appraised within a school system which long ago lost any sense of realistic purpose, the criticism index for the children reaches maximum level. But before getting into those issues in detail from Father's point of view, let's rejoin Father and Mother as they continue their swim upstream through strong currents.

6

Where is this Relationship Going?

Because of her concern with approval and happy endings Mother retains her interest in the direction her relationship with Father is taking. Now that she has children, the proper reference point is no longer merely being married, which it was when she wasn't, but a condition of apparent balance in life, mixing the rewards and responsibilities of being a woman, a wife and a mother. Her success in the first is gauged according to her personal experience and development, in the second, largely by the complex appraisal of her by Father, and, in the third, by her day-to-day competitive standing against other mothers. It is impossible to find any agreement on what makes a "good person," beyond the bare minimum of civilized behavior, while the experts appear to agree consistently as to what makes a "good parent," even though the standards may be ludicrous and one-directional. But "good wife" and "good husband" are somewhere between the extremes, where the standards are murky and variable, as the divorce statistics seem to indicate, and the debate is most torrid.

What makes a man get married in the first place? It's hard to know why anybody does anything before twenty-five. His needs for possession, actual or symbolic, are so urgent and the twenty-two-year-old is still relatively fresh from his mother's arms. What center of his life he's seeking is difficult to judge. The sex revolutionists insist that sex has been minimized as a motive because the revolution has made it possible for everyone to have enough. It still seems dubious, however, that there can be a satisfactory definition of "enough" sex for a young man in real life; his standards of judging frequency and novelty are still different from a young woman's because it doesn't have to be leading to anything for him. Sex can be pretty open-ended for him, without the distraction of worrying about the purpose of it all or where it's all going to end. The old G.I. wisdom that there's no such thing as bad sex, only good and better, was not made up in the W.A.C.

After twenty-five, as a general rule, he marries because he has to. Couples living together discover this in interesting ways, variations on a theme, but it is essentially the same for all couples. After a time she's ready to talk about getting serious. Usually he isn't and puts her off with a variety of ploys about not being sure, or what difference does a piece of paper really make, or some such. She is still under the pressures she was always under about being married, and the questioning by her mother and other relatives, especially if the young couple is living together, is ever more pointed, while her answers are ever more defensive and embarrassed. Her girlfriends, married or not, also have her under the gun because the issue of her clout with him is subtly and not so subtly raised all around, and her competitive depressions are beginning to seep in regularly. She's tried the head-on approach, complete with ultimata of various types, but he seldom budges from his irritatingly stubborn position.

What's he doing? He's testing her out, naturally, and as part of his appraisal of her he's going to see how much symbolic abuse she can take before, well, before what? Before he feels he might lose her. His positive desire to marry her is buried beneath the attention getter's chronic concern with the strategies of the game, and his constant flirtation with crisis. He doesn't respond to her straight-out verbal demands because he reads her as still being very much his woman. He finally marries in the usual case when he detects the first faint odor of defection from his ranks. A chance remark about the talent of a new guy in the office, an especially long visit to her family without constant phone calls, a certain quick look at another man at a party, whatever. The message to him is the same: a little fear, a little anger, a little marriage, now.

She recalls later that even his announcement of his wish to marry was made in a strange, take-away-the-pleasure manner, without apparent excitement or joy. She found it a bit depressing, but what the hell, that's just his way. His "joy" at getting married will generally never reach proportions worth telling the girls about, when what he's feeling isn't joy but fright that he's losing her. He marries her to hold on to her in the absolutely finest tradition of attention getting. Getting married for her is still one of the approval-seeking headline acts; for him, it's simply another step in his struggle to own her and her mind, and to hold on to them. He generally lacks the external criterion that approval necessarily supplies for her, and he realizes, despite all propaganda to the contrary, that she has to get married too, even if for reasons far removed from his. Critiques of marriage are never written by brides-to-be.

Keeping a marriage together is difficult for everybody, and once the kids arrive it's harder rather than easier in so many little ways and a few big ones. The children do provide a common center for them, but it's a terribly conflicted focus, where their motives and needs are often going in opposite directions under the facade of agreement created for outsiders. The modern stress on harmony and togetherness in marriage makes each of them intolerant of their differences in style, philosophy and values; they are each striving to have the other conform to some ideal version of married living with its many famous roles. How they deal with the discrepancy in their loving ratio, however slight, becomes an essential element of their love story; one is always slightly more in love than the other, and the love leader's policies when in command go a far distance in determining the quality of life for both as well as for the kids.

Every facet of their connection fluctuates and varies over periods of time, including their tolerance for the long stretches of boredom. Sex, which seems always to be written about as a constant, fluctuates just as widely as anything else. They sometimes go for long periods of time without touching, for a variety of stated, if untruthful, reasons. At other times, one of them feels used and abused by the other in the sexual exchange. It is nearly always Mother who feels used sexually because her approval-seeking background still has her doing things sometimes when she really doesn't feel like it or know why she's doing it. Sex takes place inside her body, not his, just as the baby comes out of her body, not his, just as his juices drip out of her body after sex, not the other way around. Father doesn't feel sexually used except in rare instances. Oh, occasionally one does meet a man who feels used in that he married a woman whose little-girl dream of adulthood was having kids with a representative husband taking his proper place; he feels that she antiseptically extracted his semen, produced two children, and that was that. But that's rare; Father's capacity to feel sexually used and abused is minimal.

But Mother often discovers that while Father has no counterpart to her alleged penis envy, he does have something that is functionally very much like her vagina: his wallet. When the people he loves are regularly getting into, not his pants exactly, but his pockets, Father is often right where Mother is when someone is using her body for pleasure without any suitable appreciation or regard. Regardless of the relative contributions of money around the family, Father's wallet retains the same sensitivity as Mother's vagina. She and the kids want his money, even for food, and Father sometimes watches with primitive outrage while the kids wolf down huge platters of goodies without a care in the world about where they came from. Often torn and conflicted by his desire to show off his success to them with money and his agony and anger at everybody's bland acceptance that he's supposed to dish up everything he has, no questions asked, Father has some interesting feelings of being used, approaching mild rape.

The sensitivity of Father's wallet seems to hold true regardless of personality type. On one end, where Father is a sport and a big spender outside, he has his moments of anger and outrage at home, so similar to Mother's feelings on the sexual issue. At the other extreme, when Father is a really cheap guy, all deposits, no withdrawals, intent on beating other guys out of a few bucks at every opportunity, his most savage torments are saved for home, where he will invent the most novel exchanges of goods or services for even a minimal penetration of his wallet. In all cases, Father is debating the same kind of issue that Mother debates sexually. What is the value of his efforts, his body, his labor, his brains? When money problems, as they are called, and sexual problems occur together, which is often the case, the vagina-wallet analogy is most accurate.

When the marriage falters, depending on what either one or both of them are willing to call "trouble," values and needs are reassessed and sometimes realigned with priorities changing or not, depending on how close they are to arriving at a common diagnosis. Just as one of them needs and loves the other more at any given time, the symptoms of distress are shown by one more than the other, although there is no direct connection between who's ahead in the love game and who is showing the signs of irritation and disenchantment. Sometimes it's the recognition by one of them that the quality of life is really lousy, but the other either can't or won't see it, or if they see it, they refuse any efforts at a remedy.

Many times their troubles are allegedly about differences in handling the kids, and presumably these differences about the children have them on the ropes. Within the range of normal behavior, this always means the same thing: the lover who is losing out to the children in the affections of the other is demanding harsher treatment of the children just to soften the sting of defeat. It's almost always Father who's demanding the change in child-rearing, and in second marriages this problem arises much more quickly. There's a better chance that Mother may also be found bitterly demanding sterner discipline if the kids were brought along by him.

But in most marriages the trouble most readily shows itself in the garden of adultery, where unlicensed bodies blend and thrash, while a spouse waits somewhere else, supposedly unsuspecting of the illicit lovers. Father goes about adultery for different reasons than Mother and conducts the game according to vastly different rules. They have different ceremonies about "knowing" what the other is up to, and the ultimate significance of the "affair" for their marriage is a complicated matter for all concerned. Let's look in first on Father's version of the sexual sweepstakes, where indeed he's quite different away from home from the way he is with Mother, although he usually plans to keep her abreast of things one way or another.

Don Juan: Father Runs Away From Home

In every city and hamlet across the country can be found bars, lounges or restaurants described by people in the business as "cheater joints," where married men can comfortably bring their paramours for a romantic drink or dinner before stealing off to a motel or to her place. At other establishments, sometimes called discotheques, but more often just "places," on any weekday evening, occasionally including Fridays, can be found hordes of men who are the very bane of the single woman's existence – married men. Married men out looking for women. They are looking for sex, of course, but they are also out to accomplish something far more important to them.

But isn't this a bit old-fashioned? After all, some of the surveys show that women can be just as lustful and eager for sex as men, so what's so difficult about an affair with a married man? Well, the jury is still out on the comparative horniness scores of each, but sex isn't the issue anyway. What makes the affair hazardous for the women that Father finds out there is not their sexuality, but their need for happy endings, which eventually gets them to wonder about the direction of it all, something which seldom enters Father's mind. The liaison has to have some meaning and some significance for her, since she's seldom able to expand her self-image or have a serious discussion with her girlfriend simply about how great the screwing was this week, with nothing past that.

When Father is out there looking for a woman, he's looking for the most appealing body he can find all right, but he's more interested in a woman who can be useful to him. When Father gets to this point, he is no longer content to simply sit around the house and punish Mother with the big sulk. By this time he knows he's not the star of her show, or at least not in the way he envisioned it in other times. Father is now vindictively vengeful and is intent on showing her how insignificant she is in payment for the unimportance she has visited on him in quite another way. Father who is out there with the girls is also usually a vain man who plans to attack Mother in the way that is easiest for him, through the use of other women. This is the position that Father reaches when he feels he has been balanced into triviality by approval-seeking Mother, and the process has increased his sulk into a towering rage.

The woman he's with? Well, she is looking for companionship too and is also seeking to gratify her approval needs and complete her life. She believes that Father has come into her life because he's unhappy and unfulfilled, because he chose the wrong mate. The notion that Father is frolicking and fornicating with her out of anger and retribution doesn't make much sense to her. Oh sure, she sometimes gets a hint of that anger, but is only willing to acknowledge that Father may have a little problem about "hating all women," probably stemming from a poor relationship with his mother.

She never sees Mother, his wife, as a flesh-and-blood woman, except in rare moments, and is generally willing to take Father's description of her and her style at face value. When the affair really heats up she's inclined to see Mother as something of an insensitive bitch who cares about nothing very important and really isn't much of a man's woman in any event. Besides, Father has a lot on the ball and if he were "together" or "committed" to the right woman, there's just no telling what kind of development and growth could flower forth. In short, her need for a happy ending, far removed from the sexual issues, has her judgment seriously clouded all along the way; to her, if there can't be a happy ending, then all that went before was useless and worth nothing.

Father, when properly motivated by the anger of watching Mother live at the fulcrum, finds such women everywhere: at work, in restaurants, while posing as a single man, on the bus, everywhere. And once the liaison is made, Father exploits her without mercy. Such affairs often go their woeful way for years, while Father invents one reason after another why he can't leave Mother just yet, including the most incredible and ironical reason of all: because of the kids. Does Father ever cheat on his gullible sweetie? Only when he can.

Again, Father is very much different away from home, far different than when he is sitting in his corner with Mother. No longer the sulker, Father is charming, often generous, gregarious, even exciting, and, best of all, he talks. Oh, does he talk! He is able now, with his new woman, to chat amiably, to explore life's mysteries, to discourse on love and to express himself with passion about sensuality and some of the new concepts about two people really getting it on with each other; that's really where it's at, man. And Father is able again to show off for his new woman; it's often been quite a while since he's really shown off with success and impact. The stories he tells now are somewhat different from the ones he told Mother, of course, but the excitement of a little awe is still there.

And how does he explain Mother to his new darling? Father generally speaks of Mother with sober sincerity, only rarely letting his anger at her bubble past his lower lip. To be quite frank about it, Father confides that he feels a little sorry for Mother; he truly hates to hurt her. He wishes with all his heart that he could love her the way she loves him, but there's just not enough woman there. If he didn't feel so damned guilty about hurting this woman who loves him so much, he wouldn't continue living with her; he realizes that it's a terrible waste of his life. To be perfectly honest about it, Father confesses, he's bored out of his wits. Since this new woman is usually a dyed-in-the-wool approval seeker, she believes this implausible tale and never gets the rage winking under the gloss of sincerity until much too late to rescue her doomed happy ending. Just how many "other women" have spent years of their lives waiting for Father to leave Mother can only be guessed, but it's more than a few.

As usual, the psychological interpretations of these liaisons are masterpieces of academic obfuscation and sexual naiveté. One major view of men who hop like rabbits from one female pelvis to another sees them as incipient homosexuals who desperately need repeated sexual conquests to keep their shaky heterosexual images intact. While this view probably underestimates the extent of the male's sexuality, it misses the range and intensity of the male anger completely. Don Juan Father is in a rage for sure, and whether his outside connections are singular or plural, he is as motivated and goal-directed as he will ever be.

The other major perspective on Don Juan Father stresses the idea that he has simply drifted into a "life crisis" or a "stage" when this kind of behavior becomes necessary to bolster his sagging ego generally. This ponderously passive concept sends Father out after some new woman as if by magic, neatly gets Mother off the hook, and puts the blame where it belongs, on immature and foolish Father. This notion is trotted out for heavy use especially when Father is forty or fifty and his affair is with a younger woman, sometimes in her twenties. In fact, Father is living temporarily in a paradise of showing off his wisdom of the world and its ways, but Mother's friends argue that Father is indeed a fool, and the aging woman's fear of younger competitors is roundly confirmed.

But what about Mother? Doesn't she have to know that Father is spending some of his time in the loins of other women for the scam to be effective? Yes and no. Yes, at a minimum she has to suspect it for the full impact of the assault to be felt, or at least to keep her coming at him in outrage and distress. No, in the sense that Father is seldom going to admit it outright until he's ready, although he sometimes tips his hand early when his anger at Mother gets quite out of control; in fact, if he gets mad enough he may even occasionally invent for her a particularly lurid sexual bout that didn't really happen. There are two situations that provide Father with the ultimate angry pleasure: when Mother and the other woman are maneuvered into a solemn meeting to discuss God knows what, with Father as the apparent prize; the other, of course, is an affair with Mother's best friend.

As usual when Father is truly angry, little of it is ever acknowledged or verbalized openly. For these special circumstances, Father now reports that he is "confused," mixed up; he just doesn't know how he feels. This uncertainty theme catches all approval seekers in their hopes for a happy ending, and the women involved try all the harder with zeal and effort to do what they know how to do. Father isn't interested in getting anything settled or resolved at all, since the profit for him is to keep it exactly where it is for as long as he can. This is sometimes carried to ludicrous extremes when Mother and her rival are in almost daily contact, neither one seemingly aware of Father's angry and punishing orchestration of the entire dance or the pleasure it is giving him.

Father's infidelity extravaganza, however, does run one very serious risk. The worst thing that can happen to Father is for Mother not to be bothered by her suspicions, or agony of agonies, if she never tumbles to what is going on at all. In the first case, Mother apparently submerges her suspicions for her and the family's own good, reasoning that in most of the visible and personal ways that count to her, Father is acceptable. Father is then left to spend the rest of his days making occasional menacing speeches about "someday," realizing that he just hit 16 with a 6.

In the second case, she really doesn't see it. She is actually paying so little attention to him that if she is finally directly confronted with the news that Father is rolling around motel rooms with other women it comes as a real revelation. When Mother is of this type she quickly dissolves into tears, inquiring at the limit of her lungs how he could do this to her and the kids. At this point Father's worst fears are confirmed, and he becomes actively divorceable at that juncture if by chance he encounters another woman who shows any substantial interest in him. Even then it may take him years to get it all accomplished because he has to stick around to punish Mother for the indignity of all indignities.

Throughout all these escapades Father has been trying so desperately to be caught. Tiny bits of mischievous evidence which could only have been left by a reckless man are everywhere. Absurdly implausible lies accompany blatantly visible artifacts, right down to, in advanced cases, the motel room key. Father's work now requires some extraordinary hours on odd days, with unusual requirements. The workaholic diagnosis itself covers more than a handful of such players and was perhaps coined by a philanderer in the first place. Mother's gullibility is tested in countless ways, depending on the state of Father's rage. The more vivid, consistent and extreme the evidence, the more apparent it becomes that Father is languishing in a gaping attention vacuum. Father has come as far down as he can come from the days when his own mother read his mind with such dizzying diligence.

In his saga of playing and punishing, Don Juan Father is attacking Mother where he perceives her to be most vulnerable, in her marriage. His behavior out in the world and the constant skullduggery about it at home have taken away her claim to have a "good" marriage, an abstract possession which has high value for Mother. Father, for a change, doesn't even mind that Mother has discussed the entire sad affair with her girlfriends and may even be getting some approval there, if not for her power as a woman, at least for her bravery and patience. Father is bound and determined to knock Mother off the fulcrum and humiliate her as far as possible in the currency he believes she understands, and that means the worth and stability of her marriage. Father often gets a savage charge out of being the bad guy among Mother's friends and family. Being the bad guy is close to showing off again, and his need to humiliate her, aided of course by her own public concept of intimacy, presses on toward objectives which often remain very obscure to Mother. When Mother tearfully inquires, "What did I ever do to deserve this?" Father, as usual, replies, "Nothing."

When the shoe is on the other foot, however, and it is Mother whose mind is absorbed with thoughts of dangerous kisses or tender midday couplings, the entire dynamic changes for Father, and radically so. The reasons for the difference in style and outcome of betrayal between Father and Mother are many, not the least of which is Father's voyeuristic needs, which seriously confound any interpretation of Mother's playing around. The expansion of the pornography industry in all of its facets yields only one hard-core conclusion: men are avid watchers. And despite every attempt by the porn-marketing folks to convince the world that times have changed and Mother is really just like father sexually, it simply won't go down. Mother just isn't much on watching, while for Father watching and doing are often neck and neck down the stretch.

Father the Voyeur: Mother Runs Away From Home

If one is to believe the writings about the extramarital behavior of the married woman, she lives in constant anxiety and guilt lest her liaison be discovered by her mate. If this is so, then Mother's apprehensions are wasted, since Father always knows when she is up to something. There is simply no way to fool Father, whose obsessional tracking system around Mother is ever alert, sensitive and suspicious of the slightest deviation from routine. Father's obsessional capabilities combined with his generous supply of voyeurism make him a veritable C.I.A. of sex. Getting Father to admit what he knows, of course, is quite another matter, as one would expect. But there are also other basic differences involved when Mother runs away from home.

In the first place, Mother becomes sexually receptive to another man when she is disillusioned and frustrated with Father's disinclination to gratify even the slightest part of her approval needs. While Mother can occasionally go for a romp on a purely sexual basis, her bedrock need is still situated in a relationship. Mother often feels that all she gets from Father, on the surface at least, are a few good times thoroughly outnumbered by constant criticism, harassment about the children, the long sulk and boredom. And for Mother, unlike Father, boredom means just that; it does not mean anger. Father in love, in the attention-getting style, is often boring, tedious and harassing to her, and she drifts toward stupefaction from ennui. Father will go few places cooperatively, do little pleasantly, and almost never praise her for any activity or service. In short, the long sulk is on, and while Mother is vexed, she is also very bored.

Secondly, Mother is seldom motivated to punish Father as he does her. If anything, playing-around Mother often feels guilty about Father and hates the thought of how much this would hurt him if he ever found out. Mother doesn't generally need revenge or retribution; she needs a lift, a new person, a new possibility of approval, someone who will correct the years of ego debilitation that Father's sulk and withholding have inflicted on her. Mother, therefore, is far more serious in her flight than Father is in his, and is accordingly far more dangerous to the marriage if she happens to meet someone who takes an interest in her. Mother is sexually legitimate too with her new fellow, complete with some real feelings, unlike Father who often leaves his new playmates feeling themselves thoroughly used, humiliated and trivialized. Father invariably believes the long sulk can go on forever, but if Mother gets lucky out there, the whole thing can end in a big hurry. Mother, unlike Father, is truly running away from home.

Father, of course, always knows when Mother is playing around, and this is so despite some impressive efforts at concealment and deception. It is simply not possible to deceive a motivated obsessive person who's made it his business to have every step of her course handicapped, even when he wasn't sure of why he was doing it. Because Mother has often not grasped the extent of Father's obsession about her and her physical location in time and space, much less his voyeuristic urges, she finds it difficult to grasp the idea that Father knows about her thing with the supermarket manager, the local golf pro, her boss or whomever. Besides, Mother is often pretty well convinced by this time that Father doesn't care that much about her anyway.

Father occasionally goes quite crazy when he "discovers" the affair, as it is generally called, but that is not simply because it is happening. The craziness is induced because he has been forced to "find out" too soon, before he is ready to confront and deal with the situation he already knows exists, even when he doesn't yet know who the man is. What Father has discovered from the depths of the long sulk is that he is terrified at the prospect of losing Mother. It is the same top-priority insight that Father occasionally makes in a hospital waiting room, with Mother perilously ill and his panic rising to stratospheric levels.

Generally, however, once Father "knows," and this is often long before the acknowledgment, and occasionally even before the act, he selects one of two courses open to him. In the first instance, once his panic has abated and he's gotten through the hazardous first weeks, he recognizes that his real priorities are Mother first, Mother's sexual fidelity second. He thereupon submerges his knowledge promptly so that for all practical purposes he doesn't know. Once decided on this course of action, Father will maintain this pose consistently and stick to it even in the face of evidence so blatant that admiration would even be drawn from Don Juan Father. Father is entirely capable of being quite chummy with Mother's new love if he happens to be in the immediate environment. While Father will sometimes even make a few nervous jokes about Mother and her friend, especially if he's part of their regular married cronies, for the most part he maintains a total dummy role. While Mother usually interprets

Father's apparent sociability around her new love as additional evidence that Father hasn't caught on, the fact is that Father is acting out his emotional priorities with a liberal dose of voyeuristic excitement sprinkled in among the love, need and terror.

The second course open to Father is one he follows if he lacks the control necessary for the dummy course. Here his knowledge is too much for him to contain, and he launches into a protracted and systematic "interrogation" of Mother, which will often last a lifetime in one form or another. Father is frightened out of his wits at the prospect of losing her, of course, but his voyeuristic needs have been ignited to white-hot intensity. His sexual fantasies about Mother are now blending with reality, and the result is often a super-obsession of single-minded dedication, which will occupy a good deal of his time until finally relieved by arteriosclerosis.

The on-the-spot interrogation takes up great stretches of time and often continues while Mother is sagging from fatigue. The apparent purpose of the inquisition is to get at the "facts" of the case and, if applicable, to induce Mother to confess. Father is now the attention giver, and Mother is having some strong reactions to this unaccustomed and largely unwelcome barrage. While the interrogation drones on endlessly, Mother struggles against a most disturbing thought that continues to pop into her head: Father wants to know all the subtleties of detail to such a degree that it's almost as if he wishes he had been there. God forbid. Mother is fighting her own feelings of revulsion and disgust very strenuously; a watcher she isn't. Father's voyeurism alone would sustain the double standard even if every other strand of it collapsed.

The outcome of the inquisition is in fact quite irrelevant. Does Father leave Mother after she confesses her sins against God and man? Rarely. Indeed, Father begins to show some rather unusual behavior himself. While he has some berserk moments, at which times he may slap Mother around a bit, for a good part of the time he seems to welcome the entire episode. He sometimes even seems to be making it easier for her. Thus, he is now willing to take the kids to the beach on Saturday afternoon; he is more docile about staying home and minding the store while Mother goes to her adult education class, which is sometimes held at her lover's apartment. Father is strangely willing to do quite a few things which heretofore had not seemed to be in his repertoire. He does not, however, abandon his investigative behavior and Mother runs into him in some surprising places indicating, sure enough, that Father is following her.

Father's sexual interest in Mother is suddenly at honeymoon urgency again, even though it may have been a very iffy thing in recent years. Of course, he's also acquired a few bad habits like talking to her about her sexual activities while they are making love, which Mother usually considers a most unusual and in-opportune time. But she has noticed that Father's pleasure in talking to her about sexual needs and activities, especially hers, has now reached approval-seeker's level of verbalization, despite these temporarily troubled times. Mother is now the center of the universe, in the attention-getting model at least, and is often confused as to what the hell is going on. Provided that she is not in love with her lover, in which case she will often leave Father anyway, Mother spends a long time adjusting to this conflicted and uneasy center-of-attention position.

Mother often allows that she is truly surprised that Father didn't walk out on her after the discovery of her affair. After all, he had told her several times over the years what kinds of things he would do to her if she ever had a sexual collision with another man, even including some spectacular physical damage. He may have even come close to his threats in the first month or so, but before long he generally has moved into a new position that Mother is at a loss to explain. "I guess he loved me all along," she concludes, and that's usually true enough, but there's still something else about his reaction that stumps her.

Father's knowledge of Mother's lover seems to excite and torture him, yet at the same time to soothe and comfort him. Father seems transported back to his childhood years, poking around at the keyhole of his own mother's bedroom, waiting and listening, trying always to see. Now that some other daddy is in the picture, even a vague and faceless individual, Father is himself again a child. Mother has indeed won and broken the sulk, and she can do thereafter pretty much as she pleases; she now has the complete child, if that is her wish. Father has recognized that Mother is the stronger and the tougher, and these are always dimensions that interest and attract him. He knows inside that when Mother decides to take her body elsewhere and use it, he becomes unhinged in a way that unemployment or cardiac fears could never accomplish.

In this never-never land of adultery Father's major emotional risk is that he cannot afford any public knowledge that he knows. He cannot face having to recognize the situation too soon, before he is able to tie it all up with some of his long-standing fantasies about Mother. Hence, Mother's often ill-advised confession is ill-advised precisely because Father already knows, and her overt statement of the truth forces him to admit something about himself and his needs for her that some men still find disgusting, sickening and eventually unbearable. Father has to be "ready" in his mind with fantasies and facts about Mother tightly, if not neatly, in place, because premature acknowledgment may panic him in a most painful and novel way.

Fantasies are funny things anyway. When Father takes the interrogation course outlined earlier, which usually features more animation and emotional chaos than the dummy course, part of the tumult is caused by the fact that Father discovers that some fantasies should have stayed fantasies. The difference between the fantasy and the reality of Mother and her lover was too great, and the reality more painful than he ever imagined. This can also be true in Mother's case. Her famous rape-and-force fantasy about this man or that seems to be another one that is perhaps best left a far piece away from reality. It doesn't seem that it would be much fun at all.

Through all of Mother's betrayal dance she's learned something about Father's need to watch and has come to appreciate Father's need to talk about sex as well. Father's combined interest in watching and talking is often featured in one version of his solution to his needs; this is called open marriage, a type of "arrangement." An open marriage is generally a connection between a threatened and voyeuristic man and an attractive woman who is kind of fond of men anyway. The key to this arrangement is that Father can't really lose Mother now, since in his mind he has defused her arsenal by agreeing to it in advance. Father can accept what's going on sexually and profit from it, provided she doesn't get serious about it or start believing that she's in love or something. Mainly, the open-marriage couple talks and talks about life, about friends, about relationships, and about other people, and Father is able to make his own personal sex-talk calls at any time of the day or night. In these situations Mother is often not clear in her mind as to the overall motivation for the whole thing, but she goes along with it anyway for the good of all. When neither Mother nor Father has much insight into their lifestyle, they are called "swingers."

All Those Sad Divorces

There are "good" divorces and "bad" divorces. A good divorce is one between a man and a woman who recognize that they married the wrong person or should never have married anybody, or even that they have out-grown each other and are vastly different people than they thought they were going to be when they were twenty-three. Good divorces are relatively rare. A bad divorce is one between two people who were pretty well matched in chemistry, who have had the most intense personal relationship either will ever have as adults, but who encountered insuperable difficulties in dealing with their different meanings of love. Bad divorces are quite common, and, taking a few liberties with destiny, should not have happened. There are many divorces somewhere between good and bad, of course, where one party flees and the other is left behind scratching his head, but they are impossible to categorize.

Father, in the classic bad divorce, is convinced, as noted earlier, that Mother does not and could not ever love him *enough*. He seldom feels that she does not love him *at all*; that is Mother's position. Because of the different goals inherent in attention getting and approval seeking, these conclusions are entirely logical from the basic definitions of these motives. Father is nearly always willing to concede that she cares about him to some degree somewhere inside her, but her attention to their children and the rest of the world has proved too much for him, and the supreme irony is that this is *never* mentioned by either of them. Father only speaks of why he fights with Mother in the vaguest terms, while Mother can be far more specific as to Father's shortcomings and iniquities.

Because Father is unable comfortably to express his jealousy of his children and the reasons for it, and he is unwilling to verbalize his anger at and needs for Mother, he often finds himself living in "near divorce" conditions anyway. This is the brinksmanship situation where one party or the other is living with a bag packed, sometimes literally, and if it's Father's turn he usually believes this will go on forever. For these couples short physical separations are a common element in their ongoing strategy, where they come apart and come together again rather routinely, often for decades.

Father feels not loved enough because he is not alone in her attention and, therefore, in her affection. It is usually long past the time for showing off very well for her, with all of its fantasized and sometimes actual rewards. He has developed a resentment and hostility toward both Mother and children, the latter expressed in "teasing," excessive or unusual discipline and rejection, and the former in the long sulk, consistent Don Juanism, or whatever antic can bring her the most pain.

The children, in particular among her activities and interests, bring Father a special anguished rage, and sure enough after the divorce, the alimony and child-support payments become his instruments of revenge. Mother retaliates by making Father's visitation as difficult and inconvenient as possible, regulating contacts and phone calls and slandering Father to the kids on a nonstop basis. Whichever one feels the most aggrieved will find reasons why the kids should know the "truth" about the other parent, and thus follows regularly some of the most bizarre dialogues of parent-child relations.

Beneath all that anger Father truly loves Mother in the way he felt a love affair should be. The bottom line for him is that Mother's attempts to please and placate him only make him angrier because she does that for everybody, and he comes off such interchanges feeling stupid and even more unimportant. It's as if each bit of attention and concern she gives him only serves to remind him of where all the rest is going, and he's off and running again on an anger binge.

Mother for her part remains convinced that he doesn't love her at all. Every visible sign is negative, and his moodiness and agitation with the children are the clincher. As an approval seeker and one used to balancing, she does not have his inevitable eye for where the bulk of his approval is going; she knows she is not getting her proper share, which depresses her, makes her dispirited and begins to enfeeble her fabled desire to please. True, she has had occasional signs that when she really gets angry back at him instead of just depressed, or when she becomes totally turned off, he comes around and is even very attentive for awhile. Since the long sulk is some extended version of the childhood tantrum, indifference always brings it down hard, making counter-sulk the ultimate weapon for Mother.

But this "success" only makes Mother angrier because the use of this tactic forces her to abandon her approval-seeking stance, which is her bread-and-butter position. When she's in a counter-sulk even the kids notice and disapprove, thinking now that it is Mother who is being "mean." In addition, getting involved in Father's nonsense clearly indicates to her that she's playing a "game," which deeply threatens her beliefs about what an "honest" relationship with a "real man" should be all about. This will never do; the emotional cost is too high. Her success with the counter-sulk causes her other uneasy feelings too.

There is an awful lot of child in Father, she reasons correctly, and, after all, who really wants the approval of a child? A child, like an old person, is a low-prestige individual whose approval has little value. Indeed, the realization that Father is at least one-half child is sometimes intolerable for Mother, whose vertical yearnings have been fed for years by soap operas at all levels. She does not recognize his harassment of her as an expression of love and need for her and a clamoring for her attention. He has *only* her to concentrate on personally while she has him and the children and even some random sources of approval. He is singular and narrow, while she has to balance that which refuses to balance, at least easily. Their conflicting versions of loving are about ready to undo them.

During the disaster, the position of the children and the expression of that position are also of prime importance. If Mother implores Father to reconsider "leaving me and the kids," or berates him for leaving "us," Father's hopes for any last-second reprieve go down for the count. With that kind of language, Father realizes again that Mother just doesn't get it, at least the way he sees it. Father never leaves the children; realistically, the idea of leaving a child doesn't make any sense anyway. Father leaves Mother, with the children by and large caught in the cross-currents of coming apart. When it's Mother who is departing, Father only uses the "leaving us" ploy or "breaking up the family" approach when Mother has connected with another man. Its use at that time concedes that he has lost her, but he hopes to snag her on whatever reefs of guilt may still be visible in the family harbor.

Families and friends are properly notorious in fanning the flames of anger and outrage swirling around the dissolving couple. Mother often and Father occasionally, have talked and complained for years about the injustices suffered at the hands of the other, and the complaints reach eager ears. Friends and others, anxious to show off how smart and experienced they are in life, are usually eager to toss in some advice and tactics along with the commiseration. The advice is almost always challenging and belligerent, even when the same script has been repeated between the lovers for years. Relatives are usually on the provocative side as well; some have been spoiling for a good fight for years and possibly for some justification in the bargain. There is seldom anyone around to suggest that perhaps there is more to this war than meets the eye.

Eventually, someone has just the lawyer for Mother or Father. In most of these situations the attorneys themselves come to be a uniquely destructive force in the disintegrating love affair for a variety of reasons. Lawyers are angered and offended when they feel they are simply part of the game between the two. "Calling my lawyer," for some couples is like "calling the cops" or "calling your mother" for some others – it is simply part of their routine. As such, it is thoroughly harmless and not to be taken too seriously, even if it's time-consuming and inconvenient. But professionals' touchiness is legend in America, especially when their position and dignity are trifled with, and lawyers are among the touchiest.

Secondly, most attorneys are an intensely practical sort and have a zeal for collecting fees that approaches a level of avarice which would make loansharks blush. Featuring what is called a "retainer," a cash-up-front system also favored by plastic surgeons, orthodontists and similar idealists, they require the couple to invest in their dissolution in advance. Accordingly, in their dedication to completing the "case," as it is called, and to get the rest of the money, they become overtly instigating agents themselves. Throwing threats and legal horror stories at client and adversary alike, the lawyers spread fear, distrust and added anger by intruding themselves as the final link in the chain holding Mother and Father together. When Mother or Father takes the eager advice to have the other speak only to the lawyer, it's all over except for the disbursements.

Years later the true sadness of this final end is often revealed to the participants, however sketchily, but there is enough residual anger and defensiveness left to make them deny it. Second marriages come and go, and even when they stick there's often a strangely uninvolved air to them, almost as if there isn't anything worth fighting about. And, of course, the divorced lovers continue to fight over the "children," long past maturity. Many young adults contend with the still-spluttering flames of the love affair. Will Father pay for his daughter's wedding? Will Mother behave herself at her grandchild's christening? Will Father come to his son's graduation? Gosh, it seems just like yesterday.

How To Have A Beautiful, Fulfilling, Meaningful, Enriching, Healthy, Joyous, Creative, Open, Closed and Perfect Marriage

Mother frequently claims that she wages a constant battle against her tendency to say "yes" to people when she really means "no." The presence of this frustrating confusion of intention may testify to the degree of her interpersonal intimidation or perhaps the ambivalence of her desires and goals. Her background training in approval seeking makes either interpretation possible, and the problem itself is a direct consequence of the approval-seeking style. Approval training with its emphasis on the "right" answer or the "correct" way, the behavior that is going to win her the approval of others, also makes her concerned about communicating with Father with a view to expediting a happy ending.

Father's problem, on the other hand, seems to be exactly the opposite of Mother's: he's often saying "no" when he means "yes." The attention getter's concern for keeping her close to him by prolonging the trouble often requires a series of negatives when, in fact, Father may be feeling quite affirmative at the time but still reluctant to give in to the happy ending and thereby let her go. Yet when Father's having big problems with Mother, some version of happy ending is essential if they aren't to come apart or dangerously close so he must sometimes say "yes" to keep the game going. His attention-getting need gives him a few advantages in dealing with Mother, but a couple of profound disadvantages as well.

One disadvantage of the attention-getting motive has to do with time: Father sometimes waits too long to recognize the danger he and Mother have drifted into, and it is often too late when he finally comes out of the obsession to note that Mother has given up for real. As a consequence, even if it doesn't happen to be too late, Father responds to a crisis in a way that Mother usually doesn't. He comes out of his obsessional fog with a bang when it finally dawns on him that Mother is headed for the door When Father is in a real crisis he can be very productive in making significant alterations in his connection to Mother.

Mother is generally able to talk about their problems at any time, crisis or no, but then her approval training limits her in the ensuing discussion. Mother has such an unrelenting certainty about what the right issues are and the right words to be used. Because attention getting does not depend on any specific language, Mother often misses the purpose of it completely, although she does sometimes catch the rhythm of it, which necessarily is of a push-pull, up-down cycle. "Why is it," she asks, "that when I seem to be feeling down, he seems to feel better, and then when I start feeling better, he starts his nonsense all over again?" Mother has captured the possessive rhythm of it without seeing the need beneath the behavior and the anger which is always there to some degree. Sure enough, in discussion with Mother, Father doesn't have all that much trouble admitting that he loves her; what he will not admit is that he's angry with her, as if he knows that once that admission passes his lips, he will also spit up all the subterranean demons that would compromise him forever. Father's strength is like glass – firm but breakable – while Mother's breadth and range make her like rubber – she bends but doesn't crack.

Mother invariably wants to talk about trust, which, as noted earlier, has a vastly different meaning to her than it does to Father. While Father winces, sometimes visibly, at each use of that word, he seldom debates its use with her for reasons known only to God. Because trust to him means that she does not want to waste time on him, he hears her chronic lament about the lack of trust as saying, "I don't want to have to worry about you or bother about you in a special way. You should be a constant in my life while I free my mind for my important job of being a mother and worrying about the kids." What he believes her need for trust is telling him, therefore, is that, while he does have a value to her, it is not number-one, that's for sure.

Since it is an obsessional, single-object motive which demands reaction, attention getting in any form is a motive which *defines the personal worth* of the attention getter to himself through the object person. Indifference, of course, assigns a value of zero and in children quickly "cures" a specific behavior but not the behaver himself, who will at the appropriate time try another from his bag of tricks.

Approval seeking on the other hand, is not an obsessional motive, is not restricted to a single object, nor does it demand a reaction; it solicits one but doesn't demand it. Accordingly, it is more of a yes-no proposition about the approval coming from any of several sources. Oddly enough, while current social folklore sees the male as consistent and the female as variable, their different needs make it in fact quite the other way around.

So, when Father hears Mother's trust speech as a statement that she really doesn't want to have to worry about him, his attention-getting need answers with, "Oh, yes you will," and he launches into one winning antic or another. Father's long-range problem is that he needs, at bottom, to be the *only* item on her mind, and she cannot possibly do that and still survive elsewhere on any human basis. Occasionally one sees a woman surrender her kids from a first marriage for the "sake" of her second husband, which comes as close as anything to the "ideal," but the later havoc for her and the children makes the cost extremely high, to say the least. In general, it simply can't be done.

Father's dilemma then moves a step downward as he decides if he can live with merely being number-one rather than one and only in her mind. It's around this issue, of course, that so much of his scrutiny of her behavior takes place as he observes and records the daily values she assigns to him and to others. If Father observes, in practice, that he really is number-one in her mind, even if it's a close race, which it often is, his attention getting remains, of course, but its cycles become narrower and the frequency diminishes somewhat; that is, he's seldom inclined to take them to the brink as often. When Father's survey of value indicates that he's trailing the field behind his competitors, the kids, her pose as a married woman, her family, her friends or whatever, then the attention getting is difficult to regulate, because there's now a need to *punish* her in addition to recapturing the straying attention.

For Mother, if she is able to see his need as not only being different from hers, but also as purposeful in determining value, as it really is, then she's in a position to read her own scorecard. Sometimes she decides that Father is really only third on her head list, and that's that; the ball is then in Father's court. Quite often she's mildly shocked to discover that he loves her in the way men love within that need. After satisfying herself that he does, she realizes that she has greater opportunities to influence their life together than her previous estimates had indicated. Approval seekers, probably because of the physical and/or emotional anxieties of having to be good during their lives, do not take readily to the "game" inherent in attention getting. They are much happier dealing with constants than having their "love" tested and determined every day or every week. Still, once she understands the rules and some of the behavior, Mother can often do a real fancy job.

Attention getting is hard for Mother to understand initially because she has little positive experience and familiarity in dealing with disruptive behavior. That she's the center of it all doesn't necessarily make her feel any better, because the need for order and happy endings has her frantic with the messiness of loving by attention-getting standards. Interestingly, Mother learns from her children that when another person loves you and needs you they make demands on you which must be reasonably met, or the frustrated demander can get pretty disruptive. She's aware that her kids have some sizzling needs for her that they do not have for Dad, at least at that temperature. But if Mother doesn't value the child enough to meet those needs, then the anger builds, turned in or out, and plenty of disturbed living may soon be the order of the day. One of the sadly over-looked facts in those custody situations where the kids go to Dad, which excite the modern-change freaks so much, is that the children do have needs for Mother, visceral and abstract, that won't be resolved by any court. They love Dad, of course, and value him the more for his efforts in their lives, but inside them they know that Mother just didn't try hard enough; try working that one out twenty years later.

Once Father and Mother come to any kind of understanding about their individual objectives, they are as free as they will ever be to appraise the narrow options. For Father, he can't be everything in her head, all alone in romantic grandeur, so his value now must be appraised against what value being number-one has and what awareness Mother shows of that. Mother has to be worried about being a mother, of course, since the world as always has her under close inspection. Her choice then seems to come down to being merely a good mother or mother of the year. If her choice is to put her energy into being mother of the year or the decade, her chances for divorce go up logarithmically.

For Mother, the perfect marriage she likely dreamed of as a girl is not to be had. Father is going to deprive her of some part of that, depending on the value reading he gets from her. His necessity to "spoil" it for her to some degree is mandatory for him if he is to salvage his value to her as primary sweetheart and lover. These days there's a particularly savage divorce that Father initiates after the last child leaves home or thereabouts, the famous empty-nest syndrome. Father has struggled along with Mother over the years and is watching when the last cub leaves to see if she is going to join up with him again, or what. When he sees that nothing changes and Mother is going to retire on her laurels after successfully raising the kids in a successful marriage, Father hits her where it hurts, in her marriage. Father is seldom going to another woman either, although there may well be one somewhere in the picture. Mother and her friends insist that it's got to do with a bad phase about younger women and sex, but that is rarely the fact of the matter. It is pure vengeance, long delayed and, in some cases, long threatened.

So, the two of them are left with the ultimate compromise of life's aspirations: he less than all to her, she with less than a perfect marriage. In the usual case, as the lovers wend their uncertain way toward the Sunset Honeymoon, the constant measurement and exchange of value appraised determines the overall ratio of good times. At the age of sixty, Father's famous moods are still actively assessing the value index, just as they were at twenty-five, he's still often denying the obvious to Mother, and he's still, especially at his most peculiar, possessive and in love.

7

The Overparenting Society: where's Poppa?

Father lives in a society which is constantly convincing itself that it is "child-oriented." To keep proving the point it seems to be necessary that the adults in question submit ever longer affidavits of service, activity, participation and what is called "helping" the child in some project or other. In short, one has to show that one is concerned with the welfare of the child and, while the presence of the child is not essential to that demonstration, the presence of the parent certainly is. Auditioning for the parent-of-the-decade award, therefore, requires the same level of energy expenditure on a sustained basis as that required for the construction of the Alaskan pipeline.

Accordingly, the one suggestion about the child which cannot be tolerated in this milieu is to "leave the kid alone." To leave the child alone translates into "doing nothing," and doing nothing as a parent in this society is variously seen as dangerous, selfish, stupid, destructive or downright hostile to the noblest standards of parenthood. What a blow to full emotional employment such a policy would be; millions everywhere would be out of work, and the bureaucracy would have to try to interest people in "less meaningful" things.

In America, parenting is an activist idea, demanding that concern for the child be shown clearly and effectively by high visibility and intense involvement. Listening to a group of young mothers talk about their children and child rearing, it soon becomes clear that a subtle but serious competition develops among them as to who "does" the most, who moves about more, who creates the most events and interactions per day, who contends with more problems, who "goes" more places, who is "on the run" more exhaustingly, much like salesmen filling out their daily call reports. The world's approval is at stake, and one dare not finish up the track in this contest.

One of the results of this philosophy is that many children are subjected to an avalanche of a certain kind of attention which fatigues them, distracts them and often makes them quite neurotic. Indeed, the point presented here is that more children have their lives warped by the excesses of overparenting than by anything that could be called underparenting. For so many of these children, it would be a blessed relief to receive a great deal less parenting than they are now getting. For a variety of reasons, few parents are eager to entertain the prescription to leave the child alone. Such a suggestion raises their anxiety level, expands the range of sincere guilt, makes them feel trivial and unimportant, and eventually makes them angry because it threatens to close down a major showing-off activity and to dry up a vast well of approval.

Now that the dynamics of Father's life with his child are at issue, it is time to explicate the meaning of the terms "parent" and "child" as they are commonly, but silently, understood in society.

While the word "parent" is generally said to be used with a non-sexual connotation, implying either Father or Mother, in fact parent means the female parent, the mother. Most books and magazines even remotely about parenting are written for mothers, and all suggestions, advice, warnings, bromides and truisms are primarily directed at them. Written stories about fathers always concern unique men in novel situations, with a kind of Ripley's Believe It Or Not flavor to them. Public lectures by mental-health professionals on any aspect of parenthood are attended largely by women. Publications for men, as noted earlier, are either about sports or naked women; lectures on parenting for men are virtually nonexistent.

The How-To-Parent business is marketed in exactly the same manner as any other in the retail industry. Mother is the primary consumer by far, and the marketing strategy is fashioned accordingly. All such publications, regardless of whether mothering or fathering is in the title, are in fact directed to approval-seeking Mother. The prose is invariably activist, abounding with volatile verbs – incessant demands to *do*. The number of helpful hints to approval seekers on how to intervene in the child's life approaches the infinite. The bulk of them consciously capitalize on Mother's competitive anxieties about her children. We certainly don't want to see our little ones fall behind the others and end up a failure, now, do we? My goodness, no, not if it can be prevented by some solid approval-generating intervention. The entire pot is sometimes frothily sauced with a suggestion or two on how to get Father more involved with the children – get them an erector set and have them build the Brooklyn Bridge.

The use of the word "parent" as a euphemism for "mother" is most important. It means that any discussion about parenting and children is largely, even if unconsciously, carried out on Mother's home turf. Father is decidedly uncomfortable in such discussions, often mildly angry and usually quite guilty. However vaguely, Father often recognizes that something alien is going on, but will often silently indict himself for not keeping up with his child's life, instead of recognizing more directly the profound semantic confusion around him. All the talk in such discussions always emphasizes doing, taking, going, and, of course, talking. Father eventually grows somber, surly and silent.

So too is the word "child" subject to similar confusion. Here again, the word is commonly said to be used in a neutral, non-sexual sense, but, in fact, the reference is almost always to a male child, a boy. Imagine a discussion of discipline problems in the home making much sense if it were not implicitly assumed that the subject of concern is a boy. Ask the schools about what they call behavior problems, and then decide if they are not, in fact, always talking about boys. How many times is a girl child called an underachiever, that vast diagnostic category reserved for recalcitrant middle-class boys who just aren't shaping up? And now that the "hyperactive child" is becoming the "in" diagnosis, don't take any bets that four out of five of them will be anything but boys, most of whom have made the fatal blunder of developing high anxiety at an early age. On the other hand, when the sexual conduct of the child is the issue, then one can be sure that, even after all the magical and revolutionary changes of recent vintage, the child in question is still young Sis.

The reported proportion of emotional and behavioral problems of boys compared to girls bears a striking resemblance to the ratio of crimes as committed by both sexes. In both cases, the vast majority is male, and some of the conclusions to be drawn are the same for both. In crime, one reads an occasional story of a spectacular female felon, which, like the unusual father noted earlier, seems always to be put forward as indicative of significant changes. When one finds a disturbed girl, she is proportionately very disturbed indeed, and generally it is found that considerable effort and energy have been spent in helping her along the path to disaster. In part, this discrepancy means that boys do receive far more attention from parents and schools alike, for various reasons, but the cost to Sonny is staggering. For our purposes, the words parent and child will only be used when there is a fair chance that they could apply to either sex in fact.

The term overparent, therefore, refers usually, but not exclusively, to approval-seeking Mother. At a guess, 20 percent of fathers are overparents but generally Father has enough trouble identifying himself in discussions of parenting; when the actual context is overparent, he is lost altogether. Overparenting is a showing-off and/or approval-seeking condition featuring high visibility in the life of the child. The premises of overparenting as a philosophy involve a set of delusions powered by an enormous expenditure of energy, personal motivation and attention. Mother's world is permeated by these delusions at every level, and while she will seldom challenge them openly, she is often in legitimate conflict with herself, way down deep.

These delusions deserve examination, one by one.

Everything In My Child's Head, I Put There

One of the basic reflex assumptions of overparenting is that the child could not possibly have any thoughts, beliefs, feelings or ideas in his entire psyche that the parent did not put there, personally and directly. While overparents are willing to acknowledge that other life forces and experiences make a difference in the child's life in the abstract, they are only able to discuss them tangibly when such influences are bad or negative. Thus, a "bad third grade teacher" is recognized as a definite negative influence because the child resumed wetting the bed at that time. And yet even this recognition of outside negative forces is a sometimes thing.

One version of this belief can be seen when a child gets himself into some trouble with the law or school authorities. When overparent says, "Where did I fail?" or, "Where did we go wrong?" deadly serious questions are being asked, full of conviction that only the parent could be responsible for such a momentous outcome, even an unpleasant one. Meetings between courts or schools and the child's parents in such situations plainly bristle with defensiveness and self-righteousness, literally oozing the premise on both sides that only the parents could have caused this failure in English or Grand Larceny-Automobile.

An even more subtle illustration of the power of this naive belief can be seen when pointing out to parents how very much different in temperament a troubled child is, when compared with his relatively untroubled brother or sister. Again, by reflex, overparent quickly responds, "I don't know why – we treated them exactly the same." The anxious assumption here again is that obviously parental treatment could be the only relevant and important factor in such a circumstance. Why it should even matter that the kids were raised exactly the same, even if that were not obviously impossible, puts the emphasis right where the overparent philosophy demands that it be.

Perhaps the prototype of this belief is best shown in the process of adoption. How does one go about creating one's own child from scratch, when in fact the child has been created for you by others? Shall we even tell the child he's adopted? Maybe, just maybe there's a chance. . . . Most adoptive parents decide they'd better tell the child. But then the child will ask questions later on, won't he? In private-placement adoptions, where the intermediary-advisor was an attorney or physician, the professional advice usually got right to the heart of the matter. "Let's kill the parents off. Just tell the kid his parents were killed in an accident, or maybe that the father died in World War II and the mother in an accident. That ought to do it." Do what? Well, wipe out the entire past and start the child entirely from the beginning, with the new parents. Down with genesis.

Even today, the adopted child grown up has more than his share of troubles should he decide to find out something about his roots. He may well face accusations of ingratitude after having been saved from the gutter. What, in fact, he was saved from was dozens of other couples who fervently wanted that baby as much as the lucky couple who got him, but the gratitude has done a 180 over the years. Society seals the adoptee's birth record in order to make the overparent concept official, and the inquiring adoptee is treated by agency and bureaucrat alike with a surly condescension normally reserved for aliens and former convicts. The legal secrecy is justified on the grounds of protecting the anonymity of the natural mother, who at the time was a frightened teenaged girl, a member of a large group not notorious for their political clout in America, with no place else to turn.

The belief is supported by the widespread notion, diligently aided by the mental-health establishment, that unhappy children must of necessity come from unhappy parents. While this is obviously true in many cases, it is certainly not so in others.

Part of the problem lies in the definition of a "troubled child," which is not nearly as self-explanatory as might appear. Then too, some of the children in question come from parents who are profoundly satisfied with each other. These are people, certainly a minority, who are both much involved in their own personal relationship and in their own personal activities. They are often people who enjoy traveling and recreation together, and as love matches go, it is hard to beat them. But sometimes they are just not interested in children, and the children know it. They are not really "rejecting" parents in the way that word is commonly used; they just aren't interested. The voluntarily childless couples of the future will largely be recruited from these ranks, to everyone's advantage.

It should also be clear that this delusion of total parental significance rests heavily on the notion that one's child is one's possession. Overparent owns the child in exactly the same way as an automobile, a house, shoes, bowling trophies and skis are owned. Ownership also carries with it the right to deal with the child as one sees fit under all circumstances. Anyone who seriously believes that we live in a child-centered culture in any healthy way for the child has only to listen to an overparent group discussing discipline to have some quick second thoughts.

The subject of disciplining children is often one of the favorite topics in the overparenting society. Father enters this area more frequently than he does elsewhere in child-rearing, always for somewhat different reasons than Mother, as discussed earlier. Such discussions of discipline, with their eerie themes of the whens and the hows, the amounts and the acceptable weapons, will quickly convince the listener that beneath the outer concern for the ultimate well-being of the child, there is the unquestioned assumption that the child is property and to be dealt with accordingly. Policemen questioning parents in child-abuse complaints are used to the response, "It's my kid, isn't it?"

It is additionally gratifying for overparent to believe that the child needs constant attention, lest a fragile psyche be warped and bent by sinister and sometimes mysterious forces out there in the world. Despite the experts' incessant warnings about the inevitable traumas outside, the average child is a good deal healthier emotionally than all the thunder would allow. Still, the overparent society clings to the notion of the vulnerable child, partly because the idea creates necessities and justifications for counter-measures and allegedly remedial techniques which, if they don't affect the child, do wonders for the parent.

To gain some perspective on the emotional health of the average child, one really has to look to situations where children live in open distress and agony. Scattered about in some form of foster care or in institutions of one type or another are children with no person claiming ownership of them and typically suffering from some major problems. Despite the shortage of babies, one could adopt a white child next week if one wished, except that it would be nine years old and blind. Similarly, in large urban ghettoes can be found some black children reeling from the impact of living with marginal people and, of course, the objective devastation of ghetto living. These are children who truly need help in the activist sense, just as do crippled and retarded children whose lives at an early age require intervention and remedial effort of a certain type. For these children to be intervened for, helped and aided is part of the meaning of being sick. To extend and justify the necessity of intervention from these cases to the average child, who isn't sick, and call it healthy parenting is one of the great sleight-of-hand tricks of our time.

The Overparent Need For Total Control of The Child

As the ego-centered belief that my child is exclusively and entirely my creation psychologically and that his emotional health demands my constant attention constitute the basic premise of overparenting, total control of that child is its objective. For overparent to control and manipulate the child is the essential goal of a great many child-rearing practices. Indeed, the objective of control goes beyond child-rearing in the home and extends clearly into that other huge area of childhood life, the school. While parent-teacher type organizations were established for many diverse motives on both sides and serve many functions, the basic expression is to show one's "concern" for the child and, thereby, to exert a little better control around the school.

Overparent's desire for control of the child is fueled basically by the approval-seeking need for the outside world to smile on her for the many virtues she's produced in her child. Observe almost any young mother in public with her child. Her eyes are constantly scanning the area to catch perhaps a smile or a nod of approval from total strangers as to how inherently appealing her little nipper is. Father seldom even looks up.

But overparent's need for control is also fed from other sources, not the least of which is the psychiatric/psychological establishment. Now, in addition to her ordinary armament of affection, discipline and guilt, overparent has scientific principles. While the psychological guru on the specifics of child-rearing has been in evidence for some time, more recently the behavior-modification people have raised the interest in child training to a high art. Because all behavior-mod principles are entirely premised on total control of the captive subject, as in prisons and hospitals, it is no accident that books and courses pushing these areas are achieving greater and greater acceptance among the overparenting crowd. Control the child for purposes of ever-more exquisite control.

There is something very comical inherent in the exchanges between the behavior-modification expert and the parents of an apparently poorly controlled boy. The behavior specialist talks in tones of almost desperate earnestness and sincerity, using such deliciously antiseptic words as "behavior," "response," and, of course, the inevitable "reward" and "punishment," those crowning jewels of total control. The parents, for their part, listening with such serious expressions, like novice students in a Latin class, following instructions intently, they themselves now being controlled and apparently experiencing little discomfort. Behavior mod means the clipboard crowd, so Mother and Father are given some daily clerical forms to carry home to chart and record Sonny's progress toward the land of the saved. Just the home a boy could yearn for. Some of the byproducts of Professor Skinner's genius have found a home a long way from the rat laboratory.

What the message of control is to the child, however, is clear: this child is not acceptable unless he is exactly the way I want him, and I am determined to leave no trick untried in order to get it. Young children themselves are only sometimes a source of approval to overparent, but their conduct and behavior before others always is, and that's where the noose gets tight. Stroll through any supermarket and watch what happens when some youngster stumbles into a display of canned tomatoes, drawing the attention of all handy observers. Mother is usually mortified and sometimes will punch him out right on the spot. Surely there must be something in the child-training book about poor coordination in messy buildings.

The inherent inadequacies of the simple reward-and-punishment system will be reviewed later. Children really do not learn that way, but even before the technical capabilities of that system are examined, the feasibility of the entire idea of control might be discussed.

In actual fact, the myth of total control can be quickly exposed to anyone willing to learn. Have a homely daughter or a frail son, have a chronically ill child or one with a speech impediment, have one son a better student that his brother, have a child with acne, have one daughter more gregarious than her sister, have one son a better natural athlete than his brother, have a short son or an overweight daughter – in short, have ordinary children, and observe the effects of their particular characteristics. One quickly learns just how much, or how little, control one has.

Consider, for example, the concept of "peer pressure," as it is often called. The term itself indicates that we as adults regard the influence of the child's companions as being an alien, unpleasant and potentially negative force. Actually the idea of peers simply recognizes the child's desire to function effectively in his natural environment with his natural companions, just as we do in ours. Are peers a strong force in a child's life? Unquestionably. Are they a good influence on the child? As often as not. Nonetheless, a mention of peers is often sufficient to send approval-seeking overparent into a diatribe about leaders and followers and similar claptrap.

Overparent generally has a violent reaction to the subject of peers. Listen to any parent who is deeply immersed in the "bad companions" number, and the control fetish is revealed in bold outline. Seldom or never does one hear about the good and helpful things certain friends may do for a child, and there are always many. Only the potentially bad is apparent to overparent, and her children's "peers" are a constant source of suspicion and jealousy for her. The obvious thing wrong with peer influences is that they are not under her control.

Physical characteristics of individual children are a vast area of uncontrolled input into a child's life. Past third or fourth grade, at a conservative guess, is it true that our world functions on beauty, or doesn't it? Is it a fortunate thing to be handsome or pretty, and is it a bad thing to be ugly or homely? Now, everyone wants to say, of course, that it shouldn't matter, but try telling that to any twelve-year-old. Children assess themselves realistically against the rest of the world and draw their own conclusions about what power attractiveness gives them with others and what status and prestige it supplies with their contemporaries. Is there a good chance, therefore, that the handsome/pretty ones develop more self-confidence than the homely ones, regardless of whom their parents might be? You bet there is.

Perhaps the epitome of futile parental attempts at control can be found in all the advice offered to parents about preparing the first-born for the arrival of the second child. Carefully applying all the control advice of the experts to make the first child a part of the process in order to make him feel better about the whole thing, Mommy brings her little helper into the scene with enthusiasm and pleasure. But, of course, the baby hasn't arrived yet. When the baby does arrive, the older child usually has the devil's own time with it. Why? Because despite our fervent desire to believe otherwise, the child is not a fool. He sees for himself that his mother is gone and is now ministering to the new baby, leaving him angry and put out. And, who knows, he may even be the angrier for having been misled for these past months about how much fun the whole extravaganza was supposed to be. It is not going to be an unequivocally pleasant event for him to be replaced as the resident infant, no matter how elaborate the preparation is.

Controlling children as an objective has usually been well integrated into overparent Mother's life style. Because of her own training as an approval seeker, Mother has a much greater need for order and neatness and that everything, including the people around her, be in the proper place and external harmony of circumstances be maintained. The language of control, therefore, reaches a receptive audience. Words like "training," "guiding" and "developing" carry with them the promise to overparent that she can get involved in every facet of her child's life with feelings of self-righteousness and necessity.

Ironically, the need for control of the child often leads directly to fragmentation, disarray and enduring hostilities in the multi-child family. Because so many of their difficulties arise between themselves, the children's first recourse is to find Mother or Father for interpretation, resolution or revenge. If Mother and Father have given up the need for control, they may choose to teach the kids that their strongest loyalties are owed to each other, not to Mom and Dad, and they had better settle their differences among themselves before risking a summit meeting where all may lose. Does this lesson change the way kids feel about Mom and Dad? Of course not; they don't take it that literally, but it resolves numerous discipline-type problems before they reach the board room. If Mother and Dad can't quit on control of the kids, then they face the prospect of informers, tattle-tales, black sheep, motivated liars and a generally hostile climate which, years later, finds the grown brothers and sisters "not very close."

Within the context of the overparenting society, what can Father do about the many features of his child's life that he realizes are largely out of his control? What's the remedy when these conditions are having negative effects? Nothing?

The only thing Father can do is to give what we professionals call support and encouragement, and this is true regardless of whether the child faces a problem or not. There isn't anything to "do" about these circumstances in any active sense. These are the kinds of things that depress children, especially the physical characteristics, but the feelings are generally realistic and the parental "remedy" has to go to the feeling rather than the fact. Can Father make some suggestions regarding the options for his child in a problem situation? Of course he can, but this is a long way from "doing" something about it in the activist, over-parenting sense.

The significance of parental support and encouragement, regardless of circumstances, without the frenzy of control, can be seen vividly today, listening to the cacophony of self-help voices which urge the reader to "learn to love yourself." Even to like yourself is not sufficient for some of the more expansive gurus who feel that true fulfillment can't be reached with such a tame level of self-fervor. In either case, that awful question is raised, which has yet to be answered successfully, "What's wrong with me?" The support and encouragement response called in the trade "acceptance," blandly enough, gave the answer before the question was ever generated. "Nothing's wrong with you, Baby, you're the best."

It should be emphasized, however, that overparent does not give up easily on the subject of control. During the teenage years in particular, overparent will often explode in a spasm of control, or rather the loss of it. Opening the child's mail, or at least finding a way to discover its contents, is routine. Eavesdropping on the child's conversations, telephone and personal, with friends becomes an accepted part of everyday life. And, of course, the "frisk," the endless searching of the child's living quarters in pursuit of some potentially damaging evidence, where indeed she sometimes "just happens to find" some incriminating item, becomes a common outrage. The national hysteria about narcotics, especially during the sixties, gave validity to search-and-seizure operations up and down the block. Teenage time is a difficult time for overparent, and the threat of loss of control, so vital in the approval-seeking operation, is truly panicking in its effect. That the teenaged children of overparent become realistically paranoid during these years should surprise no one. If Father has been participating in this viciousness, or sitting idly by allowing it to go unchallenged, it should depress us all.

The Volume Theory and the Absent Father

The idea that more is better than less is ubiquitous enough to indicate some measure of practical truth, but it certainly has some real limitations. If one piece of candy is good, then five pieces should be super – and the child gets sick. If making love once a day is exciting, then three times a day should be ecstatic – and the lovers become bored. If one shot of heroin produces an absorbingly pleasant high, then an additional shot on top of it should produce cosmic peace – and the addict overdoses. But whatever the risks of taking on too much of anything, the idea has been firmly established in overparenting.

What the volume theory means, when applied to child-rearing, is this: that a good parent is *there*, literally and physically *there*, to be seen, felt and heard by the child, and, furthermore, the more hours spent per day in such a physical condition, the better. By "better" is meant more emotionally gratifying and educational for the child, and more moral and uplifting for the parent. The final logic of this position would seem to be that if both parents and the child lived on top of each other twenty-four hours a day, then we would have the total family experience, with happiness and mental health abounding.

Now, the volume theory itself is a direct extension of the basic rudiments of the approval-seeking motive. If you are not with me physically, you do not approve of me; therefore, you do not love me. The approval-seeking overparent simply projects her own needs onto the child, has it dressed up for her in media-type psychological jargon and, presto, we have a fundamental standard of good parenting.

Seen in a slightly different context, this is a reflection of the approval-seeking Mother's endless struggle with what she calls loneliness; she simply cannot stand to be alone. After a grueling childhood training of her own in approval seeking, to be alone is the genuine kiss of death for her. To be alone means to be disapproved of, not approvable, unloveable, dead. Filled with both angry self-pity and the almost frantic need to find somebody to be with her, she experiences life disintegrating around her. Surely, therefore, her child must have the same needs.

Mother's magazines, no matter how sophisticated, reinforce the volume theory at every opportunity. An endless supply of self-pity is pumped into Mother, noting over and over again her lonely bravery in raising the children alone, while *he* is not around. One commonly cute characterization is to note all the many roles that lonely Mother fulfills in her child's life – golly, is she ever busy. Unspoken, of course, is the additional implication that she plays the role of father as well, but that is usually left to the reader's own imagination. But even with all of this spiritually uplifting activity, there is always the awful loneliness. To be left alone does to approval seekers what silence and counter-sulk does to attention getters. It destroys them.

As usual in such discussions it is happily assumed that more is better than less, as it truly must be if approval seekers are to make any sense of their own lives. Furthermore, it is often darkly hinted that were it not for the lonely, embattled mother, the children would be running the streets, becoming degenerates, or at the very least unwholesome and potentially dangerous individuals.

Now, Father has a great deal of trouble with the volume theory as applied to child-rearing. The major problem for most men is their tremendous competitiveness and fluctuating hostility toward their children. Then too, fathers of all personality types are often bored with their children and with their children's activities, but they are often unwilling to say this to the "involved" mother. Finally, many fathers are ambitious men who recognize that to get ahead, one has to be into the volume theory in his job. Accordingly, it is often true that Father's aspirations in his job or career are terribly important to him, and in overparenting terms the family, of course, must "suffer."

To approval seekers the necessary inference is created that if you are not there, again literally so, you don't care, you are a rejecting father. Rejection as an active psychological force and physical absence have really nothing to do with one another. It is ironical that real rejecters, like psychological "bad guys" of any type, do their most impressive damage when they are present, not when they are absent. Ask any battered child – they are experts on this. But you don't have to question most fathers longer than about five minutes about how much time they spend with their children to sense the depths of guilt and defensiveness that are present on this topic. The more sophisticated fathers will fall back on the obvious bromide that it is the quality rather than the quantity of time spent with children that counts, without really believing it for a second. The less sophisticated will begin to recount the number of recent purchases or the number of events they attended with the child. In short, more volume, riding the guilt express.

Implicit in the volume-theory element of overparenting is the approval-seeking notion that in all parent-child encounters it is always the parent who is *doing*, always the parent seeking out the child so as to give him some new "experience." The child, as always, is seen as the passive recipient of this attention, presumably soaking up the pleasures of all this motivated involvement. Indeed, the overparent theme requires that the child be viewed as passive property to be molded and shaped into adult excellence. The goal of it all for overparent is that she can deliver the ultimate approval-seeker's compliment to her child – the chilling "I'm so *proud* of you."

But is the child really all that passive? Not at all. If the capacity to learn and absorb new ideas and information is the basic skill in life that it appears to be, then children are in the best of all active positions. The inquisitiveness, the curiosity and the desire to learn are so intense that such students really require few teachers in the activist sense. This fact strikes a hard blow at any approval-seeking teacher because it means that she is not *needed* nearly as much as she would like to be. Indeed, the relentless curiosity of children fatigues and irritates her in addition to making her feel unneeded. An active learner simply doesn't give the teacher a chance to show what she knows and control the exchange very easily.

When a child needs a teacher, he will usually come looking for one. This is physically so in the sense that children will come asking for answers or help; you seldom have to go to them, even though one would hardly think that watching the overparent in action. But to be needed is terribly vital to approval-seeking overparent, and to insure that she is needed requires plenty of energy on her part and certainly would not be left to the judgment of a child to determine.

It is interesting to note that the words *inquisitive* and *curious* are seldom used in describing adults. Apparently the implication is that to be an adult is to have learned everything there is to learn already, and to know everything worth knowing. Of course, described differently, one could characterize this person without inquisitiveness as boring, narrow-minded, rigid, opinionated and even stupid because he never learns anything, regardless of what or how little he already knows. Because they are inquisitive, children are highly motivated learners and are far more capable of learning by themselves than the overparenting society ever credits them with. And the capacity to learn is the capacity to change and grow.

The child's need to learn not only makes many teachers expendable, it is absolutely basic to certain kinds of problems that children develop. There is, for example, a growing realization that a fair percentage of our children seem to be victims of something called learning disability. However vague the neurological and psychological genesis may be, the key behavioral fact is that the learning-disabled child's most intense problem is with *himself*. He *wants* to learn so badly, and he can't, for reasons he doesn't understand. The frustration and frequent self-hatred generated by this phenomenon is intense and has little directly to do with what anybody says to him about his problem. He personally is involved; he wants to learn and he is very angry because he can't seem to do it. If the child were not intensely motivated to learn, there would be little frustration to endure as a consequence of his inability. Few outside factors, such as grades, approval or parent-teacher conferences, can affect these feelings very substantially. The child is angry for reasons of his own.

That the inquisitive child is very motivated to pursue his own goals flies regularly in the face of the basic view of the child-as-fool premise of the overparent philosphy. While all the advice and instruction to parents emphasizes the many things the parent can and should do, the child's own needs and motives often upset the best laid plans for parental coups. If the volume theory of overparenting is taken literally, then all that time spent with the child is necessary to allow the parent to do all the many things she's supposed to do, while the child is presumably just hanging around being a fool. But Father discovers that a good deal of his parenting seems to be with the child doing one thing or another, while Father does nothing but watch the child perform, which is generally all the child needs.

A great deal of fathering, as a matter of fact, lies in doing exactly that. Father as "approving witness" is a truly important person to children, and as the approving witness Father is really called upon to do next to nothing. He only has to watch and say, "Good," or for the very enthusiastic, "Wow!" When Father is an overparent himself, he will always manage to make it more complex and thereby ruin the whole thing. A small boy on a diving board is eager to show how well he is learning to do the back flip. "Daddy, watch me, watch . . ." and then he does it.

Imagine the feeling deep inside that child when Dad answers, "That was good, but try keeping your legs closer together." Talk about missing the point. Or, his child may sidle up to Father and say in a declarative way, "Did you know that they don't have any zoos in Africa?" And Father, in the grand spirit of the overparent, says, "Well, that's not exactly true – they have wildlife preserves in Kenya." Were it not for the child's age it would be called one-upsmanship.

So much of good parenting from the child's point of view has nothing whatever to do with volume of physical presence. Past infancy and up to the age of ten or so, the child's need to learn and to show off severely limit just how much of anybody's presence is required. Motivated by his own engine, he gets what he is after and departs. All Father has to do when interacting with the learning process of the child is, for the most part, to nod affirmatively and give the approval sought. The child gets the closure he wants, and Father has fathered. Whether the performance approved of was *exactly* right would interest only overparent who needs to instruct, and by so doing to tell the child that he is *almost* O.K.

The Approval/Martyrdom Need To Believe That Parenting Is Hard

That being a parent is ipso facto terribly difficult is one of the unshakable delusions of the entire overparenting philosophy. And you debate the other side of this argument at your peril. Here the image of the child changes somewhat from passive fool to potential assassin, or, at a minimum, to a living burden to be suffered throughout one's life. This belief incorporates more than the objective control of the child, it creates the theme that regardless of the outcome of the child-rearing, the whole business is inherently hard and painful; truly a martyr's dream: no winners. This is the point where Mother's suffering with the kids meets Father's work agonies head-on in the Misery Derby. Mothers who openly admit that the whole thing was fun are as rare as Fathers who admit the same about working.

For approval-seeking parents to be able to say with gusto, "I have given my life for you," brings feelings of martyred joy impossible to duplicate elsewhere. None of it is true, of course, but that seldom matters, and the child rarely sees through it anyway. This is *guilt* country, and no one does it quite the way a dedicated approval seeker does, one who can deliver the proper lines with appropriate fury mixed with the inevitable "hurt." Approval-seeking parents are always being hurt by their children. What is *hurt*? Freely translated, it means, "You have disappointed me, you have failed me in the eyes of the world by not living up to the moral or achieving expectations I have had for you. In short, I am not 'proud' of you. You have not brought me approval."

Approval-seeking Mother does this number simply by being a mother. In other words, it comes with the station in life. In this context, all she has been "doing" for the child, all that sweat and energy she has expended, will now come home to roost to the profound disadvantage of the child. Approval-seeking Father does it in a different way, described earlier, but it is often just as effective. When both Father and Mother are into it, their children live and grow pretty much surrounded by people who, according to them at least, are out there literally dying for the kid.

In the martyrdom feature of the overparent philosophy, *effort* becomes all important. It is never merely that overparent is *doing* for the child, but that what she is doing is hard, is taking great effort. The approval-seeking motive is complete in this respect – it is not only what is done that deserves reward and appreciation, but also that the effort that has gone into the doing demands sympathetic approval from all sensitive and right-thinking people. It takes only a scintilla of skill, therefore, for overparent to convince the gullible child that all this effort is *caused* by him, and once that connection is made the sky is the limit. If the child comes off well in this exchange, he will feel merely grateful and slightly unworthy; if the child comes off poorly, he will feel vaguely villainous for reasons he can't really pin down and slightly incomplete all his life.

Of course, the more sales-oriented section of the mental-health establishment has weighed in with some strong words of their own. Read any book at all on parenting and by the language used, you can sense an urgent need to believe how hard it all is. "The most difficult job in the world," "... the momentous responsibilities of parenthood," "... the enormous burden of parenthood," are only samples of the ominous doomsday-sounding tone of these treatises. Here, for example, is a little introductory passage from one psychological company which markets a course for the improvement of family living:

> In a civilization torn by the lack of communication between father and son, and breakdown of the family unit and social structure, people are crying out for answers to the question of how to get along successfully with one another. ...
>
> At the extremes, clinical psychologists and psychiatrists tell us that over 90 percent of the problems reported by people who are mentally ill stem from the direct result of the way in which they were raised. The large majority of people flooding prisons all over the country are there because they did not receive the proper training from their parents.

How's that for torrid professional prose? It makes "this vale of tears" rather pale by comparison. But these promises of martyrdom strike a deep and responsive chord in overparent who solemnly agrees in anticipation of a life of never-ending self-sacrifice.

In the days when having children was seen as a girl's duty and obligation, it was scarcely a wonder that such a belief could be held so urgently. The pain and heartbreak of eventual loss of control of her children, which would come so inevitably to Mother, must indeed have set the martyrdom tendencies in her to whirring. Today it has changed somewhat in the precise form of the martyrdom. Overparent talks about how difficult it is to raise children in today's world, with all of its alleged freedoms and temptations and with, of course, the permissiveness which Spock launched adding to the moral morbidity of the climate. But one thing is clear in all such discussions, and that is that being a parent is hard, and nobody, but nobody, is going to say otherwise without one hell of a fight.

For the children the message again is unmistakeable – they just feel guilty about being such a "handful" to their parents, breaking Mother's heart after all that effort, while Dad keeps telling them how hard he's out there working "for the kids." The fact that children believe all this nonsense is sad because in the long run it makes them prone to repeating the same dreary song to their own children. It seems that Mother and Father both in their different ways have some awfully strong needs for sympathy, and their guilty children are the vehicle through whom these needs are expressed.

The facts of the matter again are somewhat at variance with what overparent wishes to believe. Fathering is easy. Now, many mothers almost salivate with angry agreement as to this idea. "You bet it is – for him. He's never here to do it," they say. As widespread as the notion is that men get off scot-free in child-rearing responsibilities, the whole idea that parenting in general is and should be easy is now ready for ever-increasing acceptance. And for this, as men, we should all be deeply grateful to the women's movement because they promise us at least as much liberation in this area as they do the mothers. We can confidently expect that as women's consciousness raising proceeds over the next decade to ever-widening appreciation of female opportunities, the mothers of America will find it prudent to discover fewer and fewer virtues in the mandatory martyrdom of motherhood. They are really going to want to come out of that position more and more, as they continue to learn that it is really all right if they enjoy those areas of living not having to do with children. By the time 1984 rolls around, most mothers ought to be in agreement that being a mother may not be so hard, after all. And so, how hard should fathering be? But even before the mothers are liberated, fathering shouldn't be that hard anyway.

Because there really isn't all that much to it. A great deal of it is composed of the rather passive watching of children perform, encouraging them in just about any project short of homicide, and plenty of physical touching, which, while not essential, certainly makes it easier and more fun. And a good deal of Father's time, like Mother's, is spent silently worrying about the kids, for which there isn't any cure, since Father is often reviewing his own life at the same time.

Father can spend some of his time just enjoying the many benefits that children bring him. These benefits are not to be underestimated. They can give him just about the purest love he will ever get, and children often teach him the most interesting things, if he is willing to learn. These benefits and many more can be had easily, with a minimum of time and effort, if that doesn't seem too crass. Children really do not need a man *per se* around them specifically all that much. Certainly for little children, most of what they need can be gotten from either the father or the mother.

But the need that parents in general, and approval-seeking Mother especially, have to believe that parenting is hard makes them particularly vulnerable to the final strand of the overparent tapestry. The need to believe that it is all so hard not only fashions the atmosphere of guilt and bitterness in the family, but it also creates an additional need and objective.

Parenting As A Skill: The Home As Prison

This last piece of the overparent theme is simply a belief about parenting that fits in with other beliefs in the American society. We believe in skills, we believe in technology. This isn't to say that there isn't a great deal that any parent learns intimately about the role of parent. Of course that is true. But the notion that parenting is a skill refers to the modern belief that one can become good at it, or better at it, as a matter of absorbing a set of techniques in handling children. In this respect, parenting bears a close relationship to education, where some belief is held that better teachers can be produced as a matter of learning techniques and procedures; the teachers' unions work hand-in-glove with a certain kind of parent to keep this flim-flam going even after all these years of overall failure.

This is how-to country, and the how-to market in books, magazines and courses reaches parents in some of their most basic anxieties. The overall message is that parenting is a set of techniques that, once mastered and used, will make life smoother generally, but more than anything else will make you a *successful* parent. In America one is never very far from the idea of success and failure. The entire field of how-to books by experts is premised on the promise of success and the implied threat of failure. Indeed, one of the reasons why how-to books on parenting are often bought and seldom read is that most parents become so depressed and guilty by page six about all of those wondrous things they are not already doing, that they aren't able to go on.

But let's listen again briefly to our busy psychological training course mentioned above to catch the part of the skills approach that reaches overparents right where they live.

> Everyone in our society is trained for his or her job – that is, everyone except parents. Every job in our society from the most menial to the most sophisticated requires some training period or apprenticeship. And yet the most important job in society, that of rearing children to be the most they can be, does not require any qualifications whatsoever. The lack of logic in this practice staggers the mind.

Amen! Amen! The raising of children to be all they can be – there's real poetry there.

And the idea of success is certainly where the money is to the approval-seeking parent. The logic here is that the advice being put down by the expert will lead to success with a child and inevitably approval for Mother as the parent. For her, it is even a social and approval-getting mark to have it known that she is interested and involved enough even to be attending such a course. What kind of advice is found in all the how-to stuff? It is always rife with control-and-manipulation language, always with the promise that if it's followed, you can literally produce a successful child, whatever that means. The array of techniques offered is impressive indeed.

One can learn, for instance, how to increase a child's I.Q., which will enable his parents at least to boast that he is not working up to his potential (probably where the under-achiever diagnosis started in the first place). For the very zealous, one can learn how to teach the child to read by the age of two, which will give him a clear advantage around the wading pool. Or, one can receive guidance on how to explain rationally to a four-year-old that you are about to beat the hell out of him, which certainly must make violence, if not palatable to him, at least under-standable. Or, you can be sold some materials to read to your teenagers which will insure that they won't use drugs, which certainly gets right to the heart of the problem. For fathers who are closet jocks and fear that teenage Sonny's masturbation habits will drain him of enthusiasm for the roar of the crowd, they can learn how to inform Sonny casually that masturbation is entirely normal, just as if they really believed it.

On the grittier side of life, a parent can learn how to stop the child from wetting the bed, complete with gold stars for success and a plug-in mattress, which may well blast the incontinent child right out of the bed. Or, for various feeding problems, Mother can master the technique of smiling at the child or not, on schedule, depending on whether the string beans have gone down. For the slightly unruly or erratic school performer, the folks can be taught the wonders of a token reward system which, with sufficient effort and diligent saving habits, will provide the child with fifteen additional playtime minutes with Mother, and in addition will add to the warmth of the home. For those who have their hearts set on having a "creative" child for its obvious benefits, they can receive help in pushing creativity by rewarding the child for any bizarre block-building activity.

For the verbose parent, she can be taught to talk to her child in a language that really communicates, and this has the added virtue that the parent gets to look so darn smart to the kid, since the child doesn't know what the hell he's saying in the first place. For the very ambitious and insecure, one can learn techniques on how to guide (ah! that word) their teenager to a successful career, or at least one that will impress neighbors, relatives and friends. For the intellectual crowd, they can learn techniques to stimulate their children to learn odd words, which will certainly pay handsome dividends in kindergarten. And for the really global thinkers, they can master the skills of how-to mother, how-to father, how-to uncle, or how-to step-aunt, which are more or less the complete courses.

Implicit in all of this skills business is the rock-bottom belief that the child is stupid. As always in family living, where there is an "expert" there must be a fool close by, and the child's role is the obvious one. The unconscious purpose of all this tinkering is to make the parent look smart, so it becomes almost mandatory that the child be stupid. The bottom line here can be found in "educational" toys, where the clear implication is that children even need help at playing, something at least which earlier generations were willing to grant them expertise in.

But there is a further complication in the skills-and-training approach. Psychological experts really do not know what works or succeeds in child training; we do know something about what *doesn't* work. In a symptoms-and-diagnostics conscious society, there is simply little call to develop any professional skill at understanding what produces either a normal child or a normal adult. There are few therapists around who specialize in the normal child; normal is whatever is left over after the diagnoses are counted. And, all too sadly, the very asking of many of these how-to questions indicates a particular state of mind in the parent. No amount of how-to technology could influence that very much.

Fathering is not a skill at all, it is a *relationship* between a male adult and a child of either sex. As a man, a father *lives* with a child, the same as he lives with a woman. Some of the needs are clearly different and so too are some of the mutual expectations, but there is also a great deal in common. To be a father is not a job, and if father really sees it that way, it ought to tell him that somewhere inside him he really doesn't want to see that child in this home. Or, at the very least, it is a chore, and not a very rewarding one at that.

It is amusing to note the similarity between the advice given to the activist parent and the theme of "management training" offered to business executives at all levels. If one reads the seminar brochures produced by organizations which perform these training services, one notes the muted macho theme of most of it and the overt activist philosophy in all of it. Words and phrases like, "be a pro," "get things done," "get in the game," "handle situations decisively," "get results," "be a hard-hitting executive," all have that locker-room ring to them, basically capturing the theme that if you learn how to *delegate, communicate* and *solve problems*, you will be a success and right on top. It's all skills, and what's more, it's all learnable. Learn how to motivate people, and executives are presumably taught how to motivate their subordinates. It's always "we" who motivate "them," we do it to them, presumably because "they" have no motives of their own, "they" are idiots.

The five primary delusions of overparenting have been reviewed here because they provide the major background against which fathering as well as mothering is evaluated. The overparenting syndrome is almost totally dedicated to "success" and the gaining of approval through the medium of control of the child. Because popular presentations of parenting are, in fact, always statements of overparenting, Father finds himself nearly always in an adversary position with Mother, and she is almost always his constant critic, but not vice-versa. Unconsciously, both parties realize that overparenting is Mother's thing, and because the popular themes are Mother's themes, Father is implicitly elected to be the bad guy. When Father tries to defend and alibi for his inability to fulfill what in reality are Mother's criteria, the discussion deteriorates and another three days of life are lost to absurdity.

It should be noted, however, that overparenting as practiced is truly a punishing existence for Mother. It *is* just as hard as the martyrdom need demands it to be. Days are full of high irritability which makes Mother vulnerable to the slightest chance event of ordinary living. The evenings bulge with further torment brought on usually by the school system's revenge on the community, that hallowed but sadistic practice called homework. Blessed relief finally occurs when the children are at last in bed and asleep, which really captures the heart and soul of the result of overparenting – the children are only "enjoyed" when asleep. The price of overparenting is terribly high for parent and child alike, but the pathetic vision of Mother feeling her only relief and joy of the day when the harassed kids are finally asleep should make us all wonder what insanity ever produced this – what price love?

If Father is the typical male underparent, as he generally is, it is not that he is a failure, except by overparent standards. He can make a few unique contributions to Father-child life, but in areas seldom measured and appraised and of apparently little merit according to today's frantic standards of successful parenthood.

8

Father with his Child

As we have seen fathering is by no means the simple proposition it's often made out to be. Father's preoccupation with Mother's comings and goings and the state of his attention index from her are constant obstacles to the meaningful and realistically enjoyable use of his time with the child. But even with the ever-present hazard to fathering presented by Father's love connection to Mother, Father can contribute a good deal to the child and vice versa, depending on how Father sees the entire business of living with the child in the first place.

When Father sees his task within the framework of the over-parent standards and objectives, then both Father and child are in for some rocky times. Those standards which emphasize the home as a training ground where the ultimate rewards are the approval of the outside world, will affect Father over the long haul pretty much the way they affect Mother in that the kids are most enjoyed when they are asleep. Father is probably best off marching to his own drummer here and doing it his own way, it is hoped with some degree of confidence.

While doing it his own way, Father will have to resolve one of the current experts' bromides immediately, and that is that Mom and Dad should strive to be in agreement on all aspects of child-rearing. This is not only impossible for two intelligent people to do, but its practical utility is highly questionable anyway. The children are always smart and quickly figure out which one is the easy mark and which the resident warden, which of the two is quick to forgive and which one takes it all personally, and which one has no stomach for harsh punishment and life sentences and which one rather enjoys it all. These differences are not readily reconcilable, nor should they be; in actual practice, the differences all too often boil down to one parent claiming moral superiority over the other anyway.

This is easily seen in the aftermath of angry divorces where the child is contending with different people with different standards of good conduct and civilized deportment. Quite often the separated former lovers both complain bitterly about how the child is handled by the other, each leveling the charge of moral and cultural degeneracy at the other, while the child in question adjusts to each of his worlds fairly readily. It is always found that the same moral competition was going on during the marriage and it didn't have all that much to do with the kids then either.

So for Father to make his unique and important contributions to his child, he might best be guided by a few principles designed to make it all a bit easier in the doing and directed to the goal of making Father-Child living more enjoyable. Child-rearing cannot really be done by rote or a list of principles but, having conceded that, let's list a few practical awareness concepts which will help.

1. Good Parenting Is Not in the Techniques, It's in the People

More and more in recent times, research comparing various styles of child-rearing come to the conclusion that they have produced no discernible differences in the children. What actually cancels out the effects of philosophies, regimes and policies is that when considered in isolation from the individuals employing them they have no meaning. This is even true in the area of physical punishment; there are people who love their children and punch them and there are people who have some very ambivalent feelings about their children and also punch them, and the children reflect the difference. The upshot of it is that there are good people to live with as a child and some who are not so good; exactly which philosophy parents should espouse doesn't seem all that important. As in all games, it's the final score that counts.

2. No Parent Is a "Good" Parent with all Children

The notion of good and bad parents as an across-the-board-proposition with every type of child at all times is psychologically unlikely. Some parents, for example, are excellent with infants but can't handle them when they get mobile. Some are fine generally with little kids but come unstrung from their personal needs when the kids become teenagers. Some are quite the opposite, being touchy and impatient with little ones and quite O.K. with them when they are bigger and more nearly adult. Some parents are fine with girls at most ages but have serious problems with boys at any time. Sometimes it's the other way where the parents can enjoy the more physical kind of life boys provide, but are sexually terrified about dealing with girls. There are parents who do rather well with their own but fall into complete disaster being a stepparent, while for a few others, intriguingly, quite the reverse is true. There are parents who do the job most effectively as long as they have a mate with them but doing it alone finds them in rapid collapse, and there are those, interestingly, who find doing it alone easier than when in tandem. There is scarcely anyone around who does it well, by any standards, at all times, at all ages, with either sex; sooner or later one's own weaknesses and idiosyncracies are reached and the parental performance becomes erratic and uneven and sometimes seriously troubled.

3. *Leaving the Child Alone Is* Not *Doing Nothing*

As noted earlier, leaving the child alone is rapidly equated in overparent country with doing nothing. Highly anxious people have real trouble doing nothing because it makes them feel depressed and useless. But leaving a child alone from the activist point of view has some substantial advantages. Consider two of the current favorite goals in child-rearing annals, toward which a parent is encouraged to "help" his child: creativity and independence. A moment's reflection should convince one that neither of these highly valued characteristics could possibly be *taught* in any direct sense, yet, advice can be found for a busy parent to get in there and help the child develop them. The facts of the matter are that creativity of thought and independence of personality are allowed or permitted to happen, even perhaps encouraged, but hardly taught, by anybody. To try to teach them is a contradiction in terms. What makes them both so rare, in part at least, is that so few can allow them to develop. Here is one of the many areas where Father as the approving witness can contribute something to his child in subtle ways without pushing the kid off the stage with all that self-serving help.

4. *Much of the Time Spent by Adults and Children Is Boring for Either or Both*

Divorced Father is often accused by divorced Mother of unfairly purchasing the affection of the children by loading them up with toys and playthings during their times together. This competitive interpretation is, in fact, seldom true. Divorced Father buys those toys because he is often bored with the kids and does the easiest thing under the circumstances by buying them things to play with so he can watch the ball game. There is still some general reluctance in parenting circles to admit that there is a great deal of boredom, mixed in with the beauty, of time spent with children but, nonetheless, it is frequently the case whenever any one of us is not with our natural peers. Of course, the children are often bored with adults as well, and the acceptance of that is just as hard to come by. The overparent manuals can concede a child's boredom with the imprisonment brought on by a rainy day, but bored with the parents? Not just yet.

5. *The Continuing Curse of Childhood Is Not Fragility But Incompetence*

Parents often worry about their "mistakes" in child-rearing and the possible effects on the child's mental health. As long as the mental-health model so dominates child-rearing such concerns will continue to be justified because the psychologizing of family life makes the concept of the fragile child the obvious one. But the ongoing dilemma of childhood is not fragility at all, but *incompetence* at every age from one to twenty. It is incompetence at this task or that which infuriates the impatient parent; it is incompetence which arouses the mean spirited ones, and incompetence which exasperates those with great expectations.

Whatever the child has learned and mastered at any age, there will always be a long way to go in some areas; he is always incompetent somewhere, and sometimes in several places at once at any age. One would imagine that the word "immature" began in psychology to mean a child who was very good at being a baby and playing, but who came up short socially or in school, never the other way around. The child's chronic incompetence, therefore, makes him extremely vulnerable to the standards, values and showing-off needs of the people he lives with, who generally expect ruthless progress. Thus any child is "dumb" at any age in the sense that there are things that haven't been learned yet but whether the dumbness in question will have any emotional meaning will depend on whether the child lives with great geniuses or not.

The most visible instance is in a home where one or both of the parents is what is called a "perfectionist," meaning a highly anxious person who needs complete control of every task they are involved in, who will allow no one else to help in any significant respect, because what matters most is that it be done "right." Unless the perfectionist is relieved by some humor, which is unlikely, the child's incompetence becomes immortalized, and the only issue left to be resolved is whether the child should feel merely "stupid" because he can't get out of his own way, or feel that he's "bad" because he can't do anything which satisfies himself, much less do it right. One standard individual the self-help books are talking to is precisely that sort of person; someone who simply can't find a way to feel good about himself because his childhood incompetence and failures which were once objectively accurate but could have been emotionally insignificant have now been cast in concrete.

6. Children Always Learn Two Things Rather Than One

So many parents are delighted when some behavioral technique or other "works" and some irritating or incompetent habit of Sonny or Sis is brought under temporary control. But the simple behavior-consequence concept is not really complete in practice; it studiously underestimates the overall capabilities of the learner. The children always learn two associations: one specific and one general. This is not simply a principle of childhood learning, but applies to all creatures, adult and animal as well. The rat in the box learns to press the bar within fifteen seconds to avoid the punishing electric shock to its feet. Sis learns that she can get two pennies or tokens for hanging up her coat, one for throwing it on the couch, or none at all for the tossing-it-on-the-floor number. But later, try petting that tame rat, or try getting Sis to show a little generosity, and my, my what they have learned.

Even when performing correctly, they have both, in their different ways, also learned the values of their world and the people they live in it with: hostile, controlling and slightly sadistic. Which association will prevail in the long run, long past the age-relevance of the behavior in question? Three guesses.

Children of divorces learn a number of things simultaneously about Father from what would appear to be a fairly singular set of circumstances. If Father picks them up on a weekend and returns them at the designated hour, they know that Father doesn't live with them anymore, for sure. If Father picks them up and takes them to his place for the day, they learn that Father has a real other home which they visit with him during visitation times. But if Father picks them up and takes them to his place, moving them in and having them sleep overnight, and keeping some of their possessions there permanently, no matter how small his new place may be, then they have learned that they have two homes and that they don't "visit" with Father, they live with him. They have learned Dad's desires and feelings about them in each case exactly right; they have learned something about Father, regardless of what verbal input they have had from anyone else.

The second or additional association made in every "simple" exchange always concerns the character of the adult or the climate of the place that's in the air. If Father wonders which of the associations, the specific rewarded or punished behavior or the symbolic and broader one will last longer, he might speculate about some of the bosses he's had during his career. In every case, Father learned what performance brought reward or censure from a given man, what activities brought outstanding appraisals or had Father hurriedly sending out resumes. But Father also learned that a few of these men were characterized in male jargon as pricks, which means an authority who could not ever be trusted, regardless of appraisals or rewards, and that was not learned in any specific encounter; that was just learned.

7. *Good Fathers Have Good Children*

What does any man actually believe a child is, any child? The popular overparenting philosophy invariably sees a child as passive property to be shaped and molded toward his "potential," capable of eliciting approval from the world, or as a devious and treacherous assassin who is constantly at work dreaming up new ways of harassment or plots to deny his struggling parents their hard-earned approval. The principle here is an important one and a profound one: as you see them, so they are.

If Father sees his children as enemies, they will be enemies, if he sees his children as burdens, they will be burdens, and if he sees his children as good, they will be good. No father can *make* a child good; one can only see and appreciate the goodness that is there. If Father feels the approval need to prove his child's worth, it will be a long, hard life for all concerned.

One always knows that children have drawn a pretty fair hand if their father, when asked about his children, replies simply, with no anxious barrage, no superlatives, no litany of accomplishments, "They're good kids."

Index